THE END OF THE AMERICAN CENTURY

THE SLOW DEATH OF GLOBALIZATION

MICHAEL VILKIN

TAMARA VILKIN

Formatted by LiberWriter.com

CONTENTS

We live in a fast society. A large majority of us like everything fast —fast food, fast cars, quick service in a restaurant, and quick answers in the game Jeopardy. We are a Jeopardy nation. We're conditioned to answer questions like, "what happened?" and "when did it happen?" quickly, but we rarely stop and consider why it happened or what can or should be done in response.

Since 1970, our standard of living has stalled. It looks like our economy hit an invisible brick wall. That much is clear. We all know what ails our economy: poverty, unemployment, economic instability, to name a few. But what are the root causes of these diseases? And what exactly is the cure? President Trump started trade wars. Is he right?

To answer these questions, we need to learn basic economics. There is no other way. The good news is that this book was written to give readers a maximum amount of knowledge in a minimum amount of time. There is no empty talk. You will learn the root causes of our economic diseases, what exactly is the cure, and what exactly we, as educated voters, should demand from our elected representatives in federal, state, and local governments.

You will learn about our financial system—what money is, how money is created and how it is destroyed, how the instability of credit causes instability of the economy, how the financial elite is profiting from economic instability, and what kind of change we should demand from politicians. We will discuss problems of Social Security and the retirement of baby boomers, lack of affordable housing, the need to build modern cities with modern public transportation, and the best way to finance it. There are ways to improve American capitalism and to make America a better place, but only educated voters can achieve this.

WHAT IS MONEY?

Before money, people used barter to exchange goods and services. There was great need for some kind of a common form of currency, against which all goods could be priced. People started to use silver coins for purchases and later gold coins were introduced. They found it much more convenient to sell a chicken for a silver coin—and to later use that coin to pay for something else—than to carry around that poor chicken.

Silver and gold coins were commodity-based money, because silver and gold were existing commodities. What turns a commodity into money? Silver and gold coins represented precious metal commodities with established value, and it allowed merchants to use the coins as the standard measure of value. Since commodity money was readily accepted by sellers of goods, we can say that silver and gold coins at that time represented claims against the whole wealth of the area where those coins were accepted.

Many people believe that with silver and gold coins there was no inflation. That is not correct. When Christopher Columbus was trying to find a shortcut to India, he and his crew discovered America instead, where large deposits of silver were found by colonists under the Spanish crown. Spain minted a large quantity of coins from silver found on the American continent. When the amount of money in circulation increased, prices also increased. This was inflation.

What is inflation? Is it an increase in the supply of money? Or is it only a general increase of prices? There is no consensus among economists of different schools, who never agreed about the definition of money, let alone anything else. For our purposes here, we will use the generally accepted standard that inflation is the broad increase of prices across an economy over time.

THE DEVELOPMENT OF COMMERCIAL BANKING

Historians say commercial banking got its start in 16th century Europe. Among the wealthiest and most security-conscious were the goldsmiths, whose highly valuable inventory was guarded in the strongest vaults. Individual owners of gold coins paid goldsmiths to "rent" storage space in those gold vaults to protect their wealth.

Goldsmiths recognized that gold coins deposited in their vaults were seldom ever withdrawn, and that idle gold created opportunity: if the goldsmith pays a depositor five percent interest and lends that money out to a borrower at 10 percent interest, the goldsmith keeps the difference of five percent as income. By doing so the goldsmith acted as a *loan broker*, but not as a banker. We will see the difference in a moment.

When a customer put his gold coins on deposit, the goldsmith would give him a note that stated that the bearer of this note had, say, 100 coins on deposit, and the goldsmith owed him, say, 105 gold coins on a certain date in the future. Let's pause to emphasize that only one side is in debt: the goldsmith owes 105 gold coins to the depositor, but the depositor does not owe anything to the goldsmith.

Goldsmiths were acting as middlemen between lenders and borrowers. Goldsmiths had such a good reputation that the depositors' notes started to change hands as money. A buyer would pay not with real gold coins, but with the depositor's note. The seller would accept the depositor's note, go to the goldsmith and exchange the note for real gold.

That was the first step in the creation of a banking system and the evolution from commodity money to paper money. Then came a development so extraordinary, it profoundly changed the world economy: borrowers started to accept loans in the form of depositor's notes.

How did this happen? Imagine the following scenario: A borrower asks a goldsmith to give him a loan. The goldsmith lends the borrower 100 gold coins. The borrower writes a promissory note, promising to pay back 110 gold coins one year later. Now the borrower is not happy because the gold coins are too heavy to carry around, and they can be stolen. Why not deposit the gold coins with the goldsmith and get a depositor's note, which, for all practical purposes, is as good as gold? So, the borrower deposits borrowed gold coins, and the goldsmith writes a depositor's note stating that the bearer of this note has 100 gold coins on deposit with the goldsmith.

We should note that this transaction created mutual debt. First, the borrower received 100 gold coins, and the goldsmith received in return a promissory note that the borrower will pay 110 gold coins one year later. As a result, the borrower owes 110 gold coins to the goldsmith. In the second half of the transaction the borrower deposits 100 borrowed gold coins back to the goldsmith, who now owes the borrower 100 gold coins.

With time, it became customary to borrow money by accepting a depositor's note. In return, the borrower would write up a promissory note pledging to pay back the principal amount of the loan plus interest. When the borrower paid for something, the seller would usually accept the depositor's note. The real gold coins—owned by others——were stored in the goldsmith's vault, collecting dust.

THE FRACTIONAL RESERVE PRINCIPLE OF BANKING

It was a golden discovery. Now goldsmiths could make additional loans with those gold coins that were collecting dust in their basement. Most of the borrowers were accepting their loans in the form of the depositor's note, and not in the form of real gold coins. But some borrowers for whatever reason were borrowing real gold coins and not a piece of paper. Also, when borrowers paid with depositor's notes, some sellers would bring those notes to exchange for real gold coins. For these reasons prudent goldsmiths were keeping a certain amount of gold coins in reserve to meet withdrawal demand.

Was there any magic formula for calculating how many gold coins to keep in reserve? That is very unlikely. Simple logic suggests that the higher the possibility was that people would bring many notes to exchange for real gold coins, and the higher the amount of money on those notes, the more real gold coins a prudent goldsmith would keep in reserve to meet withdrawal demand.

As we see, even very prudent goldsmiths were keeping only a fraction of outstanding loans made with the depositor's notes in reserve. We should assume the goldsmiths understood that if too many people try to exchange their paper notes for gold coins, there would be not enough gold coins to meet withdrawal demand. But as long as people were not demanding gold, the goldsmiths were happy to keep only a fraction of outstanding loans in reserve. Economists refer to this as a *fractional reserve principle of banking.*

Modern banking is very different from banking in the 16th century, but if we look beyond computers, at the core, there is still this centuries-old principle of fractional reserve. It is only after the goldsmiths started to use the fractional reserve principal that the business of loan brokering started to evolve into the business of banking.

SEEDS OF INSTABILITY

Now, let's take a close look at how bank credit affects the economy. When people deposit money in their account in a bank, two things happen. First, the amount of currency in circulation is reduced, but money supply is not. Second, bank reserves increase.

Let's recall now how goldsmiths were making new loans using other people's money. When people deposited their gold coins with the goldsmith, the gold coins ended up in the basement collecting dust. When the goldsmiths were making new loans by writing depositors notes, the borrowers were leaving the goldsmith's shop with money in their pockets. Their depositor's notes stated that they have money on deposit. For all practical purposes money and a deposit were created simply by entering into a business contract, where a goldsmith makes a new loan, and the borrower promises to pay back the principal amount of money plus interest.

The interesting thing is that most people borrowed what was basically a piece of paper, but were obligated to pay interest in gold or silver. If most people borrow paper, will they be able to pay their interest with real gold coins? Will there be enough gold coins in the economy? And what will happen if there are not enough real gold coins in the economy? Let's try to get to the bottom of this.

Suppose, one person decided to borrow one hundred gold coins from a former goldsmith, who is now a banker. The banker wrote a depositor's note stating that the note's bearer has 100 gold coins on deposit. The borrower wrote a promissory note promising to pay back 110 gold coins one year later. Suppose now that the borrower bought a horse and paid for the horse 100 gold coins. The seller of the horse accepted the depositor's note as payment for the horse. The seller then went to the bank and exchanged the depositor's note for a hundred gold coins. So far so good. The depositor's note is as good as gold, but the borrower is obligated to return 110 real gold coins. The borrower may work for the horse seller, earn 100 gold coins, and pay them back to the banker. But where are the additional 10 gold coins going to come from? The problem is not that the borrower has to work to earn additional 10 gold coins. The problem is that the borrower increased the amount of money in circulation by 100 gold coins when he borrowed them from the bank, but when he pays back 110 gold coins, then 110 coins will be taken out of the economy.

Every loan reduces the amount of money in circulation when it is paid off. Suppose, for example, that a person borrowed 100 gold coins from a bank. Money supply—this is the same as the amount of money in circulation—increased by 100 gold coins. One year later the borrower paid back to the bank 110 gold coins. The money supply is thereby reduced by 110 gold coins.

The obvious question is, "if everyone has been reducing our money supply, how come we still have a lot of money in circulation?" There are a few reasons this is so. First, every bank has expenses. If a bank loaned 100 gold coins and was paid back 110 gold coins, it means that the bank earned 10 gold coins. This is income, but not profit. Income minus expenses equals profit. Every bank has expenses—buying or renting a building, paying salaries to their clerks, etc. When the bank pays salaries or rent, money goes out of the bank into the economy, and money supply increases as a result. If a bank had income of, say, 100 gold coins, but paid out, say, 60 gold coins for expenses, its profit is only 40 coins.

The second reason is that when a bank earns profit, that profit is added to the bank's own capital, and the bank will be able to make new loans with its own capital. The bank might decide to invest money in the building of new offices. Either way, money goes into the economy, and money supply increases.

In the following chapters we will be discussing an extremely interesting and controversial subject—instability of the economy. There are quite a few schools of economics: Keynesian, Monetarists, Supply Side, etc. Each school of economics has different explanations for the instability of the economy. The so-called Austrian School of economics has a deep distrust of paper money. They argue that paper money causes most of our economic problems—inflation, instability, etc. We will discuss the most relevant economic school of thought later in the book, but since we are still discussing commodity-based money, it would be reasonable to take a close look at the major points of the Austrian school's philosophy.

The first major belief of the Austrian school is that the very existence of paper money causes inflation, because governments around the world are tempted to print more paper money. We already know the discovery of large silver deposits in Latin America, or, in what used to be the colonies of Spain on the American continent, caused inflation. The second major belief of the Austrian school is that the existence of paper money is the major cause of economic instability. We will have a good discussion about instability later in the book, but for now let's answer the following question: What will happen to the world economy if currencies of major economies are backed by gold, which is called the Gold Standard? The answer is that with Gold Standard, gold is money. Countries with large deposits of gold will be digging it out of the earth and will be minting gold coins. Gold producing countries will be prospering at the expense of everyone else.

ECONOMIC INSTABILITY

The history of the world economy is a history of instability. Economic downturns follow economic upturns, and vice versa. We should note that all major economic depressions happened while the world economy was on gold standard. But—and the Austrian school has a point here—the true Gold Standard ceased to exist as the banking industry came into existence.

Let's recall how goldsmiths evolved into bankers. When goldsmiths acted as middlemen between lenders and borrowers, they were not creating new money. But when goldsmiths started to use fractional reserve principle, they started to use paper money.

When borrowers accepted loans in the form of depositor's notes, they knew that those bank notes represented gold coins, and were redeemable for them at any time. Banknotes were as good as gold. That is how paper money came into existence. As soon as this happened, the true Gold Standard ceased to exist.

Banks were making loans by issuing paper banknotes, they were issuing new money because the banknotes could be exchanged for real gold—or so people believed. In reality, the fractional reserve principal means that not all bank deposits can be exchanged for real money. For example, if a bank made loans totaling 2,000 gold coins, but has only 1,000 gold coins in reserve, it means that the bank has only (1,000: 2,000=.5) 50% of outstanding loans in reserve. The more paper loans the bank made the more interest it would collect in real gold coins, so the banks had a very strong incentive to make as many loans as possible. The only danger was that some people were taking real gold coins, and sufficient inventory of gold coins always had to be kept on hand.

If people somehow had learned that a bank did not have enough money, it would have resulted in a run on the bank. A run on a bank means that too many depositors are trying to make cash withdrawals. When a run on the banks occurs, the bank will not be able to meet withdrawal requests. There are simply not enough real gold coins in reserve. In that case, for the bank there's only one course of action: to ask borrowers to bring back the borrowed money. There is a term for it: to call loans in.

When a bank calls loans in, the borrowers are obligated to sell their assets in order to pay back the loans. Many of the bank's clients will suffer losses, and some of them will find themselves bankrupt.

If there are runs on many banks, the whole economy will be damaged, and an economic depression becomes a very real possibility. An economic downtown may take the form of either an economic recession or an economic depression. Centuries ago, people might not have used economic terms like recession or depression, but the point here is to demonstrate what happens when banks make too many loans and leave too little currency in reserves. Today we use paper money. But the basic principles are the same. Like centuries ago, the fundamental principle of banking is the principle of fractional reserves. It sounds fancy, but the meaning is very simple. It means that if too many clients who have deposits try to withdraw too much cash, the bank will not be able to meet withdrawal requests.

But what did banks do centuries ago when their reserves were getting dangerously low? Of course, they would make fewer loans, but continue to collect debt. It's just common sense. We can also assume that banks would make more loans when the economy was good, but restrict lending when the economy was bad. When banks loan freely, the economy benefits. When banks are too low in reserves, they restrict lending, but continue to collect debt. The economy enters a downturn. In a bad economy, banks restrict lending even more, and the economy worsens.

SUPPLY AND DEMAND

Supply and demand are the most important concepts in economics. Both concepts can be defined either in terms of quantity or in terms of monetary value.

Supply can be measured, for example, in terms of quantity of ice cream that manufacturers are selling at a certain price, or in terms of the total price of ice cream offered at a certain price.

Demand can be measured in terms of quantity of ice cream that buyers are willing to buy at a certain price, or in terms of total amount of money that buyers are willing to pay for ice cream at a certain price.

A *market price* is determined in the process of negotiations between buyers and sellers. When sellers reduce the price, buyers, in most cases, are willing to buy more. For example, consumers are buying a certain quantity of ice cream at a certain price and spending a certain amount of money. If the price of ice cream were lower by, say, 50 percent, the consumers would buy, probably, twice as much ice cream at that price. This means the quantity demanded at the lower price would increase by 100 percent, the demand in terms of money would stay the same because the consumers would pay a price that is 50 percent lower.

At $10 per gallon of ice cream consumers might demand a hundred gallons. If the price of ice cream is reduced by 50%, to $5 per gallon, consumers might demand 200 gallons. This means that demand, in terms of quantity, increased 100 percent, from 100 to 200 gallons, but demand, in terms of money, did not change because a $10 per gallon demand in terms of money was ($10 x 100) $1,000 and at $5 per gallon demand in terms of money is the same ($5 x 200).

If the price of ice cream goes up by 50 percent, from $10 per gallon to $15 per gallon, demand in terms of quantity might drop 30 percent, from 100 gallons to 70 gallons. But demand in terms of money will be ($15 x 70) $1,050, which is almost the same as before.

As we see, when the market price goes up, quantity demand goes down, and when market price goes down, quantity demand goes up. In both cases demand in terms of money may or may not change.

THE BUSINESS CYCLE

In the second half of the 20th Century, the American economy experienced economic downturns approximately every 10 years. Economic recessions took place in the following years, plus or minus a year or two: 1950, 1960, 1970, 1980, 1990, 2000. The so-called Great Recession started in 2008, but it felt like a full-blown depression.

Economic instability is the most important subject in economics. Economists of different schools offer different theories about the causes of instability and various solutions. The theory of business cycles is one of the most widely accepted approaches. According to this theory, a business cycle consists of two parts: an upturn and a downturn. During the first part of the business cycle employers make investments to increase production, hire workers. This causes an upturn in the economy, which lasts a few years. At some point the expansion of the economy slows down because, according to this theory, there is overproduction of goods. Overproduction means that there is not enough demand in the economy, and manufacturers start reducing production. As a result, many workers lose jobs. When workers lose jobs, they don't have income to buy goods, and this causes demand in the economy to drop even further. The economy enters a downturn, which is the second part of the business cycle. A short downturn in the economy is called a *recession*. A long and severe downturn, when millions of people lose jobs, is called an economic *depression*.

According to this theory of a business cycle, the main problem is overproduction of goods, and the only logical and practical solution is to reduce production until the excess inventory of goods accumulated in the warehouses of manufactures is sold.

The theory of a business cycle, or economic cycle, does not explain why there is suddenly overproduction and the lack of demand. Why workers manufacturing different goods cannot suddenly afford to buy goods produced by the economy? We will start investigating this problem. We will start from classical economics - it is very easy - and continue up to and including the Great Recession.

A SHORT OVERVIEW OF THE MAJOR SCHOOLS OF ECONOMIC THOUGHT

The science of economics is not an exact science like, for example, math. Very few things can be easily proved in economics because it is a social science. The most important topics in economics are still hotly debated. Before we start our investigation of economic instability, a short overview of major schools of economic thought will help us to understand what they believe and what they don't.

When Adam Smith wrote about "an invisible hand of the free market" in his famous book *The Wealth of Nations*, he established a cornerstone belief of the classical school of economic thought. The whole foundation of the classical school is a belief that an invisible hand of the free market will always right whatever is wrong in the economy. Classical economists understood that the economy was inherently unstable, that from time to time there were economic recessions and depressions, but they believed that government intervention would make the situation even worse.

Why did they believe this was so? Because the creation of the classical school was founded upon the theory of the business cycle. They observed that during economic downturns, unsold goods were always accumulated in large quantities in warehouses. There were simply not enough buyers, and too much supply. The verdict was brutally simple: overproduction. The solution? Just wait until the goods accumulated in warehouses are sold. Manufacturers will manufacture goods in lower quantities, many workers will lose their jobs, and there was nothing anyone could do. That was the nature of the beast: the business cycle. Overproduction during an expansion of the economy, and after that underproduction during a contraction of the economy. An economic boom, then an economic bust, then, hopefully, there would be a boom again.

We call this school of economic thought "classical" because it has dominated the science of economics for such a long time. The classical economists understood that during economic downturns there was always an imbalance between supply and demand. They could not see any way to stimulate demand during economic downturns. Their solution, and their advice, was just to wait until excess supply was sold—and no government intervention.

In October of 1929, the stock markets of the United States crashed, and the Great Depression started. It was not a garden-variety downturn in the economy. This economic depression was literally crushing the bones of the economy. Millions of workers were losing jobs, millions of families did not have any income. It was an indescribable tragedy.

Witch doctors of economics chanted whatever witch doctors chant, but the new reality did not fit the old myth. The classical doctrine states that a free market will always cure all the ills of the economy with its invisible hand, but there was no demand. Manufacturers were reducing production, but goods could not be sold. Those who were unemployed did not have income to buy anything. Those who did have jobs were reluctant to spend money, because they could lose their jobs any day. The economy was dead in the water, but president Hoover was telling the country that economic recovery was just around the corner.

In February, 1933, with FDR elected but Hoover still in office, there were runs on banks. Many banks failed and closed their doors. The life savings of millions of people were lost. It was the worst moment of the Great Depression. It was clear to everyone that classical doctrine had failed. What went wrong and what was the solution?

In 1936, economist John Maynard Keynes published his famous "*The General Theory of Employment, Interest and Money*." The main thesis of General Theory centers around the idea that when the free market fails, the government must stimulate the economy by spending money and creating jobs. Looking back, it should be clear to everyone that the main thesis of General Theory is intellectually lame if not outright fraudulent. The deception is not so much in what was said as in what was not said.

It was American economist Irving Fisher who first described the debt-deflation spiral: the mechanism of economic depression. In a few words, the deflationary spiral is created when there is this imbalance between supply and demand. Low demand causes lower prices which cause lower manufacturing activity, which causes loss of jobs, which causes loss of income, which causes still lower demand, and so on down the deflationary spiral. Irving Fisher also described the reduction in money supply as the result of debt being paid off. This is extremely important, as we will see later.

Neither Irving Fisher nor Keynes were the first to recognize the importance of demand in the economy. The concept of supply and demand are the cornerstones of the classical school of economics. The greatest achievement of Keynes is that he argued in support of government spending to stimulate the economy, but herein is the deception, hidden in plain sight.

A monetary system based on the Gold Standard is fundamentally different from a monetary system based on paper money. Today governments do print money to stimulate the economy, but in 1936 the whole world was on the Gold Standard. How could the federal government stimulate the economy by spending money it did not have? There was only one way.

The only option was for the federal government to borrow money from the banks. But the banks did not have reserves to make loans to anyone, as most depositors closed their accounts and stuffed their gold coins into mattresses during runs on banks. In order to force people to deposit their gold coins into banks FDR issued a prohibition of private gold coin ownership unless they are on deposit in the banking system. The prohibition worked like magic. Owners of gold coins deposited them in their bank accounts, creating what is called primary deposits. Those gold coins became bank reserves, against which the banks now could make loans, to the federal government or otherwise, by creating secondary deposits.

As we see, FDR's prohibiting Americans from owning gold coins was much more important than Keynes' thesis about government spending. Banks would make more loans against increased reserves, and the economy would recover on its own, without increased government spending and public works. But the federal government has created millions of jobs in public works, the economy improved and the Keynesian school of economic thought came into existence. We should also note that the idea of public works was not an original idea. Public works have been utilized by the government of England in Ireland during the Potato Famine, even though the result was rather discouraging.

It is still debatable whether America's economy would have recovered on its own, without public works. If we accept the argument that the main problem after the run on banks in 1933 was the lack of bank reserves, we should come to the conclusion that FDR's prohibition did solve the problem, and the American economy would have recovered on its own, without public works. Banks would have made loans to the private business instead of the federal government, and the economy would have recovered.

When banks make loans to businesses, new money is created, as we already know. New money is spent to make investments, to hire workers, and to increase the production of goods. Workers earn wages and spend their income to buy the goods. In such a scenario inflation will be low because workers produce goods which are delivered to the market. When workers produce goods, it increases supply. When workers spend their income, it increases demand. For the economy to function normally there should be a balance between supply and demand. Whenever there is an imbalance between supply and demand, either inflation or deflation will occur.

An economic downturn is like a disease of the economy. Keynes made a diagnosis: low demand. He offered a solution: stimulate demand with government spending. But low demand is just a visible and recognizable symptom of the disease, and not the disease itself. To stimulate demand with government spending means to treat the symptoms, but not the disease. This is a major hole in the Keynesian school of economic thought. Which became clear after the Monetarist school of economic thought was created by Milton Friedman.

Before we start looking at monetarism, let's answer the following question, why has the world accepted Keynesianism as a gospel truth, when in reality it is such a defective and deceptive theory? The right answer might be that the world was so badly battered by the Great Depression and disappointed with classical economics that economists were happy to accept Keynesianism as a new religion. Government spending created millions of jobs. The economy recovered. The miracle did happen. It became an article of faith. You either believe in the new religion or you don't.

Monetarist theory attributes great importance to money supply, or, in other words, the amount of money in circulation at any given time. Milton Friedman has been recognized as the founder of the Monetarist school of economic thought, but we should note that he did not start it from scratch. Irving Fisher was the very first economist to describe the economic depression that started in 1929 after the stock market crash as a *debt-deflation spiral*. Why is it a debt-deflation spiral and not simply a deflation spiral? A good explanation is in order.

Inflation and deflation have been a part of economics ever since goldsmiths discovered how to make loans by writing a depositor's note. Was it inflationary? There is no doubt about it. More money chasing the same amount of goods will always cause a general increase in prices. But why should there ever be deflation?

When goldsmiths made loans by writing the depositor's notes, the borrowers received not only money, but they also incurred debt. New money was created with new debt. When banks collect debt, money disappears from circulation and appears again in the form of bank reserves. Liquidation of debt always causes liquidation of money. New money is created with new debt, and money is destroyed when the debt is paid off.

For some strange reason classical economists never paid much attention to money supply. It might be that they had no doubt that the "invisible hand" would correct any and all imbalances in the economy. They simply could not recognize that the liquidation of debt was the main factor causing deflation and economic depressions.

An argument can be made that when banks collect debt, they increase their reserves. With increased reserves the banks can make more loans, increasing money supply in the economy. Granted, in that case the banking system would never cause much instability in the economy. Now, let's imagine for a minute that banks make many loans for a few years until their reserves are dangerously low. These few years will be inflationary. When reserves are too low, the banks start to liquidate debt—and money. They collect debt, but make very few new loans. The result is always deflation and a recession or a depression. Rapid change in money supply is the main cause of economic instability.

Irving Fisher was the greatest economist of the 20th century. He was the first to describe the mechanism of the Great Depression, the debt-deflation spiral. What is the meaning of debt-deflation? In general, inflation means increase, and deflation means decrease. Debt-deflation means deflation, or liquidation, of debt. The word "spiral" here is a metaphor for the economy which is moving downward in concentric circles. Fisher described the process as a spiral with nine interconnected "circles."

1. Debt liquidation leads to distress selling.
2. Contraction of the deposit currency (bank deposits).
3. A fall in prices.
4. A fall in the net worth of businesses.
5. A decline in profits.
6. Falls in employment and output.
7. Loss of confidence in banks as many banks fail.
8. Hoarding of cash.
9. Disruptions to interest rates.

These are the nine circles of hell in the debt-deflation spiral. As you already know, banks start liquidating debt when their reserves are low, or when there is a possibility of runs on banks. When banks call loans in, businesses are obligated to sell their assets, which leads to distress selling. At that point the economy is on the first circle of the downward spiral. The seventh circle tells us about loss of confidence in banks as many banks fail. Hoarding cash means that people, bluntly speaking, stuff their money in mattresses instead of keeping it in banks. As people close their accounts and take cash home banks suffer loss of reserves. With diminished or depleted reserve banks cannot make loans. Borrowers have to pay very high interest rates. The economy has reached the ninth circle of hell. As we see, Fisher has described the whole process of the debt-deflation spiral in great detail. FDR knew what exactly was wrong with the economy when he prohibited Americans from owning gold coins unless they were deposited in their bank accounts.

Fisher also explained that during deflation "each dollar of debt unpaid becomes a bigger dollar." This is because the liquidation of debt causes prices to fall faster than the debt was liquidated. "The very effort of debtors to lessen their burden of debt increases it, because of the massive effort of the stampede to liquidate." Paradoxically, the more the debtors sold their assets in order to pay their debts, the more they owed.

Irving Fisher has built the very foundation of the Monetarist school of economic thought, but for some strange reason all fame and recognition, and the Nobel Prize, were given to Milton Friedman half a century later. For half a century Keynesianism was the dominant religion in economics. Irving Fisher's brilliant explanation of the main cause of the Great Depression was ignored and suppressed, and continues to be ignored today. The interesting question is: who is interested in suppressing and ignoring Irving Fisher's Theory? And who can profit from economic instability?

WHO PROFITS FROM ECONOMIC DEPRESSION?

We can go back a few centuries and theorize on what the goldsmiths-turned-bankers would have done at a time of depression, when the prices of assets were falling. Were the bankers smart enough to know a good opportunity when they saw one? If the bankers were lucky enough to buy great assets at very low prices during an economic depression, would they not benefit again from another depression sometime later? If we assume that bankers would be interested in having an economic depression from time to time, how difficult would it be for bankers to create a depression?

We already know that the fractional reserve principle allowed bankers to make loans with bank notes instead of real gold. Having received from depositors, say, 10,000 gold coins on deposit (primary deposits), a bank could make loans in the amount two or three times larger by writing bank notes stating that the borrower has money on deposit (secondary deposits). As the banking system continued to develop, bankers and their clients started to use checks to transfer money from one account to another.

Here we should note that checks are not money. Checks are instruments used to move money from one account to another. As the banking system developed fewer and fewer people were using actual gold coins for transactions. There are two aspects of this development. First, it allowed the bankers to make still more loans with less reserves, to collect more interest, and to get richer. The second aspect is related to instability of the economy.

Suppose, for example, that there were a few banks in the city, and they had, say, one million gold coins in total of primary deposits. With a fraction of loans, or a fraction of secondary deposits in reserve the bank could create, maybe, two million or three million gold coins on paper in secondary deposits. But when people started to use checks to move money from one bank account to another, bankers were able to make, maybe, five or six million in loans with only one million in reserve.

Now, imagine that banks in a certain city made loans totaling five million gold coins with only one million gold coins in reserve, and the increase in the total amount of loans was gradual—it took 10 years. We can be sure that those 10 years were very good for the economy in that city. Money supply was increasing gradually, prices of assets were increasing, and everything was just fine. But at some point, the banks could no longer increase money supply by making loans because they had already reached the maximum amount of loans for their level of reserves. The banks start to collect debt, but make very few new loans, and that is the first circle in the debt-deflation spiral, just as Fisher explained so well. As we see, before deflation of debt there was inflation of debt when new money was created with new debt. It may sound counter-intuitive, but accumulation of debt leads to economic prosperity, and liquidation of debt leads to an economic depression.

What is the lesson here? Irving Fisher's analysis makes it clear that economic stability cannot be achieved if the economy is first pumped up and inflated with debt for a period of time, and then —poof! —the hot air comes out and the bubble of money and debt burst. But, tragically, the whole history of banking is a history of economic instability, recessions and depressions, and indescribable human suffering.

Let's take a quick look at the two economic depressions that happened before the Great Depression. We will see what is common in all economic depressions.

History tells us that the depression that started in 1873 came after the prosperous years following the end of the Civil War. The depression lasted six years. By 1877 there were three million unemployed. Wages of those still employed had been cut almost by half. There was deflation. The banking panic started on September 18th, 1873, when the banking house of Jay Cooke in Philadelphia failed and closed its doors. Twenty years later, in 1893, the next banking panic started the next economic depression. Four hundred banks closed their doors. The depression lasted four years.

It was commonly believed that all economic depressions were caused by overproduction. The business cycle theory says that when there is overproduction, it means that there is too much supply, but not enough demand. This imbalance between supply and demand causes a fall in prices, or deflation. At lower prices production becomes unprofitable unless manufacturing businesses are able to reduce their cost for labor and raw materials. The economic downturn lasts until the "excess" of goods is sold, the reduced supply is again in balance with demand, and after that a new upturn in the economy begins. This is a very neat theory of classical economics—and is very persistent. Even today we see some talking heads on TV explaining that the last recession, the Great Recession, happened because too many houses were built. That is a variation of the same old theme: overproduction.

When the Great Depression started in 1929 this classical theory of business cycle caused by overproduction and the following slowdown of the economy was the dominant theory of economic instability. The deception—if it was, indeed, a deception and not honest ignorance—can be found in not what the classical theory of business cycles says, but in what it does not say. Strictly speaking, the classical theory of the business cycle is true. The only problem is that the classical theory does not tell the whole story. When Irving Fischer did tell the whole story with his debt-deflation theory, Franklin Delano Roosevelt used it to restore the monetary base of the banking system, but the debt-deflation theory was mostly ignored by the world while the new religion of Keynesianism was accepted with great enthusiasm. The interesting question is, was there an "invisible hand" which suppressed Irving Fisher's theory of debt-deflation, but promoted the new religion of Keynesianism? Let's take one more look at both theories and compare them with the classical theory of the business cycle.

Irving Fisher built his debt-deflation spiral theory on the foundation of the classical theory of the business cycle, but he explained what the root cause of an economic depression was: the liquidation of debt, which caused a contraction of the money supply, or, in other words, a reduction of the amount of money in circulation. This constant contraction of money supply is, indeed, the most important factor among the root causes of the Great

Depression. Milton Friedman had documented that at the lowest point of the Great Depression the money supply had contracted by an amount of one-third.

Keynes also built his theory on the foundation of the classical theory of the business cycle. His only major improvement on the classical theory of the business cycle was his insistence that without government intervention the depression would last too long. Just like any other classically trained economist, Keynes recognized the imbalance between higher supply and lower demand but, unlike others, he argued for government intervention and government spending as a means of increasing demand. The main difference between Irving Fisher's debt-deflation spiral theory of depression and Keynesianism is that the debt-deflation spiral theory gives us a comprehensive understanding of the root causes of depression. This knowledge can be used to prevent economic depressions in the future before they begin. Keynesianism, on the other hand, only advises increasing government spending when the economic downturn is already in full bloom.

The economic depressions that started in 1873, 1893, and 1929 came after economic booms fueled by "easy" bank credit. In the 1920s, the U.S. economy was so good that those years are referred to as Roaring Twenties. The Great Depression is a good example of what goes wrong with the economy after a bank credit-fueled boom and what the root causes are.

During the Roaring Twenties bank credit was loose. New money, as always, was created with new debt. It is counter-intuitive to look at money this way, but most of the money supply was lent into circulation. As we already know, the accumulation of debt in the economy creates prosperity, however temporary it might be. The stock market was booming. Millions of people were becoming rich, or so they thought. A short explanation is needed here about stock market savings.

During the Roaring Twenties America had paper money—dollars—but they were readily exchangeable for gold, just like many centuries ago banknotes were exchangeable for gold coins. As long as not too many depositors came to withdraw cash from their accounts everything would be just fine.

Suppose now, a person has savings in the amount of $10,000 in his bank account. With the stock market booming the person decides to get rich. He opens an account in a brokerage firm and buys 1,000 shares of a certain company at a price of $10 per share. The brokerage firm advises him to buy another thousand shares on margin, which means on credit extended by the brokerage. One year later the price of the share increased to $15 per share. Our stock investor goes to his bank and borrows another ten thousand dollars using his stock market gain as collateral. It was common practice during the Roaring Twenties. As banks were making new loans against stock market gains, the borrowers were investing the borrowed money in the stock market, which was pushing stock prices up, which increased stock market gains against which banks make new loans, and so on in a debt-inflation spiral. Let's take a close look at this process.

At first glance, it seems that when one person bought stocks on the stock market, he paid a certain amount of money, and that amount of money was no longer available to buy stocks. To understand the point, let's compare purchasing stocks with purchasing regular goods. When a person buys a manufactured product, the amount of money paid goes to the retailer, and part of that goes to the manufacturer. Money does not disappear, it just changes hands—or bank accounts, but the quantity of goods for sale is reduced as goods are sold.

When stock market investors were buying stocks during the Roaring Twenties, the quantity of "goods" of the stock market was not reduced after the shares of stock changed hands; the shares purchased were staying in the stock market, on the supply side. With regard to demand it was even more interesting. When prices of ordinary goods increase, demand for them decreases. This is one of the basic laws of economics, but when it comes to stocks this basic law works in reverse: the higher prices go the higher the demand.

As stocks changed hands, the money borrowed from the stock buyer's bank was moved to the stock seller's bank, where it would become a part of bank reserves, against which the bank would make a new loan to stock market investors. The banks were creating new money when making new loans to buy stocks. As stock prices increased the mad crowd would increase demand for stocks. The increased demand would push stock prices higher, which would inflate stock market investors' gains, which would allow banks to create still more money with still more debt, in the debt-inflation spiral.

When the stock market was booming, it seemed that the music would never stop, but it did. The collapse of America's stock market prices on October 29th, 1929 was not the end of the bad news. As stock prices declined the stock brokers generated margin calls, which mean that investors must either add money to their stock market account or sell their stocks and pay back the amount of money borrowed from brokers. It was distress selling, the first circle in the debt-deflation spiral, caused by liquidation of debt. First, it was stock market brokers who started liquidation of debt owed to them by stock market investors. As investors sold their stocks, prices fell further, which caused more margin calls, which caused still more selling, and so on in the terrifying chain reaction. As millions of investors sold their stock at a loss, millions of families lost their life savings. Thousands of stock market investors who borrowed money from banks could not pay back their loans. Facing a bad economy, banks attempted to protect themselves by collecting debt but not making new loans. For any individual bank it was a rational decision, but for the economy it spelled disaster. Liquidation of debt in the banking system was the first circle in Irving Fisher's debt-deflation spiral.

Fisher's theory of the debt-deflation spiral suggests that before the debt was deflated, or decreased, it was inflated, or increased. In other words, before the debt-deflation there was debt-inflation. During the Roaring Twenties debt-inflation came from two sources: stock brokerage houses and commercial banks. The interesting question is, did stock brokers and banks know that such inflation of debt, with most of the money going into speculation in the stock market, would end up causing or contributing to an economic disaster? There may have been thousands of small banks in the United States, and those that made loans against stock market portfolios surely did not know that they were helping to inflate a monster. But is it logical to assume that members of a few great banking dynasties, where banking expertise was passed down from grandfather to father, and from father to son, did not know what they were doing?

The fact is, economic depressions provide a great opportunity for buying assets pennies on the dollar. Congress recognized this fact. In 1934, the Glass–Steagall Act created a strict separation between commercial banking and investment banking. The logic here is unmistakable: if commercial banks are allowed to have investment departments or to own investment banks, then the largest commercial banks will have an incentive to knock the economy down into an economic depression from time to time and to profit from them. Well, today the largest commercial banks again own investment banks and brokerage houses. Should we be concerned? We will continue this discussion after we finish with monetarism.

As we already know, the monetarist school of economic thought was built on the foundation of Irving Fisher's debt- deflation spiral theory. The main thesis of monetarism is that money supply, or the amount of money in circulation, determines what will happen in the economy. If money supply is increasing too much, there will be inflation; if money supply is decreasing, it most likely will cause a recession, which is defined as a fall in gross domestic product in two consecutive quarters; if the money supply is allowed to fall significantly, it will cause economic depression.

Milton Friedman famously accused the Federal Reserve of allowing the money supply to fall too much in the first few years after the stock market crash. This fall in money supply, the monetarists argue, caused the Great Depression. The assumption here is that the Federal Reserve did have the ability to increase money supply. Let's take a closer look.

First, we need to understand one very important thing. Suppose, there is an economy with a monetary system based on gold coins. For simplicity, let's assume that the whole population of the country is just one million people, and there are only one million gold coins in the country. Suppose now, over a long period of time the population of that country increased from one million people to 10 million people, but the quantity of gold coins did not increase for some unfortunate reason. Would the economy of that country grow with a population increase by a factor of ten, with the quantity of gold coins remaining the same?

If the banking technology is the same, the economy of that country would be constantly depressed, because a growing economy needs a growing money supply. If the monetary system is based on gold coins, the growing economy will force banks to keep in reserve smaller and smaller fractions of loans. When it comes to the point that banks keep in reserve only, say, 5% of loans, then the monetary system is no longer based on gold coins but rather on paper money. We should note that such a monetary system is inherently unstable, because if even a relatively small number of depositors show up to withdraw cash, the reserves of the banking system will be gone.

The simple truth is that the Federal Reserve did not have any means of increasing the money supply significantly, and there are two main reasons for that. The first reason is that the Fed had neither the legal nor the moral power to print billions of paper dollars and make loans to banks. At that time paper dollars were backed by gold. The Fed could not print "counterfeit" paper currency based on the slim chance that the banks would just borrow the paper and never pick up the real gold coins.

The second reason is that deflation of debt started immediately after the stock market crash when the stock brokers began margin calls. The result was that millions of people who lost money in the stock market madness were in effect moving bank reserves from their banks to stock brokers' banks. The total amount of bank reserves would not decrease, but banks, even those with a lot of reserves, were not willing to make new loans in a collapsing economy. In other words, even if the Federal Reserve could make loans, the banks would not make many new loans. Everyone in the banking system was scrambling to collect debt from the borrowers.

Milton Friedman should have known that it was commercial banks, and not the Federal Reserve, that caused the money supply to drop by almost a third. Yet, he chose to accuse the Fed, and not the commercial banks. It makes the whole theory of monetarism, and Milton Friedman himself, intellectually suspect.

There is no doubt that Friedman knew the whole truth better than anyone else. Why did he not tell the truth? Most likely, it was more convenient to tell the world a limited version of the truth. In doing so he avoided the necessity of further explanation. Why, for example, did Congress enact a strict separation between commercial banking and investment banking in 1934? What exactly was the mechanism used by the largest commercial banks to profit from the Great Depression? Did commercial banks make loans to their investment departments or to the investment banks they owned to buy assets pennies on a dollar while refusing loans to the struggling economy? Milton Friedman did not answer these questions.

During the Great Depression it was recognized that big commercial banks could profit from the economic depression. It was very simple. Just don't make loans, starve the economy with lack of credit, knock the economy down into economic depression, and buy assets pennies on the dollar. By 1934 this practice became so widespread that Congress enacted the Glass-Steagall Act, which prohibited commercial banks from owning investment banks. It was one of the best laws in history of the United States. The fox was separated from the hens. The banks slowly increased credit, and the economy started to recover.

During the Clinton administration, commercial banks were again given permission to own investment banks. About a decade later the Great Recession started, Wall Street brokerage houses suddenly found themselves either bankrupt or close to bankruptcy. The official explanation was that everyone on Wall Street lost money on subprime mortgages, but no one explained where the money went. Simple logic tells us that if one side lost some money, then the other side gained the same amount of money.

Strangely enough, no one admitted making money on subprime mortgages. Creative accounting is an art, not a science. Wall Street packaged low quality mortgages into highest-rated investment opportunities, sold them to the whole world from

England to China, and everyone, including the sellers, lost money. Is it possible? Actually, it is possible - if Wall Street bought overpriced mortgages from big commercial banks.

As Wall Street's brokerage houses found themselves bankrupt, the Federal Reserve engineered the solution to save them: the largest commercial banks bought the brokerage houses. At the present time we find ourselves in the same situation as before the Great Depression. The big banks again own investment banks. The brokerage houses are perfect investment banks because they are allowed to buy economic assets for their own accounts. Money can be borrowed from their parent companies—big commercial banks. Only one thing is missing: the economic depression and low prices. The fox is again in charge of the hen house. The only question is how much time it will take before the feathers start flying.

There exist many theories explaining the main causes of economic instability, and we will discuss a few of the most interesting ones later on, but now let's dig just a bit into the cyclical nature of the economy. We already know about the business cycle theory created by classical economists. According to the classical theory, economic downturns are caused by overproduction, and the economy should recover when "excess" goods are sold and supply and demand are again in some kind of balance. It is implied in this kind of reasoning that overproduction is some kind of a cyclical event as inevitable as a day after a night or a summer after a winter.

Economic downturns are usually mild and short, but once in a while we get a real depression, just like we get an occasional long, cold winter. The banking industry encourages this kind of reasoning which is misleading and takes attention away from the real cause of instability—the debt-deflation spiral as explained by

Irving Fisher. But before the debt is deflated it must be inflated, and we should accept this fact as an axiom.

The interesting question is, how does the banking industry manage to promote false and misleading theories while suppressing Irving Fisher's theory about which we never hear? It is often said that those who do not learn from past mistakes are bound to repeat them. If we believe that the Great Depression was just a rare cyclical event which occurs only once in a hundred years, then we should get ready for another Great Depression to start around 2029. We have only a decade left to educate the population about the real causes of instability in the economy.

In the next chapter we will discuss what the top management of the banking industry will do to knock the economy into a depression, what they are already doing, and what we, as voters, should demand from our elected representatives in Congress as well as from the President of the United States.

CHAPTER TWO
BASEL AGREEMENTS

For many years now, representatives of central banks of the major world economies have been meeting in Basel, Switzerland, to discuss ways to reduce economic instability. Over the years they reached three agreements: Basel I, Basel II, Basel III. There is a lot of confusing and misleading information related to the Basel Agreements. Our newspapers write about excessive leverage, low capital ratio, and so on. There is very little information that could be used to understand the real goals of the bankers.

First, let's translate the banking jargon into simple language. The contemporary banking system and the banking system that existed hundreds of years ago have one fundamental thing in common, and it is the fractional reserve principle. We know what it means. Banks make loans by opening an account and depositing the amount of the loan in the account. The borrowers get check books to make payments. When clients write checks, money is moved from one account to another account.

In the Middle Ages people did not want to use gold coins. Today individuals and businesses do not want to carry around loads of cash; everyone is using checks and credit cards to make payments with borrowed money. The green dollars are stored somewhere in the bank basements, and they are used to meet withdrawal demands. At the present time most banks keep in reserve just 10 percent of their loans, which means that banks owe ten times more than they have in reserves to their clients. The truth about bank reserves is very simple, but newspaper articles make it appear very complicated.

Leverage is just another word for debt. Excessive leverage means that the bank owes money to creditors. Very often banks borrow money on the capital market to increase their reserves. By "capital ratio" the newspapers mean the same thing as "bank reserves to loan" ratios. Equity means owner's equity, which means bank's own capital as opposed to primary deposits, against which banks make loans and create secondary deposits. Very often, newspaper articles talk about equity to support assets (loans), but they mean bank reserves.

The stated goal of the meeting in Basel is to increase stability of the world economy. Now let's take a close look at the proposed solutions to increase the stability of the world economy by 2020.

The first measure is to increase, gradually, for a few dozen of the biggest banks in the world, what newspaper articles call capital ratio but we know to be bank reserves.

At first glance, it is a good idea for the world's biggest banks to keep more currency in reserves to meet withdrawal demands. But after close examination we will see unintended—or intended—consequences of doing so.

As we know, ever since goldsmiths discovered a way to loan 200 or 300 gold coins with paper while keeping only 100 real gold coins in reserve, banks have always tried to make the maximum amount of loans with a minimal amount of reserves. At present, the biggest banks of the world keep only about 10 percent of the amounts they have loaned in reserves. If by 2020 the banks are obligated to keep in reserves, say, 15 percent of loans, it will cause a worldwide economic depression. This is a very serious statement, and we should prove it and dispel any remaining doubt.

Suppose, a bank made loans amounting to $100 million, and the bank keeps $10 million in reserves to meet withdrawal requests, which equals 10% of the total amount of loans. Suppose now, the bank is required to keep 15% of the total amount of loans in reserve, and this must be done gradually by the year 2020. The bank now has no choice but to collect debt without making new loans. Let's take a look at how much the money supply will decline if the whole banking system increases banking reserves from 10% to 15%.

First of all, where will the banks get the additional currency to add to the reserves? If one or two banks are required to increase their reserves, then the currency would have to come from other banks. But if all banks attempt to increase their reserves by 50% —an increase from 10% to 15%—it is mathematically impossible as most of the money is already deposited into the banking system.

This means that the bank in the example above, which has $10 million in reserves, has no way to increase its reserves from $10 million to $15 million. How about issuing long-term bonds? Again, if one or two banks issue bonds to raise capital, it would be fine. But if all banks start issuing bonds, they will be chasing capital like a dog chasing its tail—a lot of activity with no result.

There is only one way for our bank to meet the requirement: to *decrease* the total amount of loans so that $10 million in the reserves equals 15% of loans. Let's calculate how much the total amount of loans will decline. It is a given that $10 million – 15% of the total, which is 100%. The bank has to decrease the total amount of loans from $100 million to $66.6 million, which is 33% less. Interestingly, money supply in the United States decreased during the Great Depression by the same percentage. At the lowest point money supply was almost one-third lower than at the highest point before the decrease. If a drop in money supply by one-third caused the Great Depression, should we just hope that this time it will be different?

Another rule proposed to supposedly increase stability of the world economy is to require the biggest banks to support assets (loans) with greater proportions of equity in order to provide a cushion against declining assets. Equity means owner's equity, or, in other words, shareholders own capital. Let's take a closer look at what it means.

Suppose, 10 people invested $10 million to start a new bank. That is owner's equity, or shareholders' equity, or owners' capital. Commercial banks accept deposits which are referred to as primary deposits. Owners' money and depositors' money become the bank's reserves, against which the bank makes loans and generates so-called secondary deposits. Both types of deposit are obligations of the bank. If the bank makes good loans, income from fees and interest will be greater than expenses (salaries, equipment expenses, etc.), and owners' equity will increase. If the bank makes bad loans, the bank will have losses instead of profit, and owners' equity will decrease.

What would an optimal amount of owners' equity as percentage of deposits be, both primary and secondary? This question is very debatable. If a bank is paying higher than average interest to depositors, the bank will attract a high volume of deposits, and it will make the owners' equity small in terms of percentage. Suppose, for example, that 10 people invested $1 million total to start a new bank. If the banking regulators create a rule that owners' equity must be not lower than, say, 10% of deposits, or loans, the bank can make loans in the amount of only about $10 million, because $1 million is 10% of $10 million. If the bank is allowed to keep the owners' equity at only 1% of loans, then the bank can attract $9 million in deposits in addition to $1 million of owners' equity, and with $10 million in reserve, the bank can generate $100 million in loans assuming that bank reserves should equal 10% of loans.

Suppose now that an average bank has $1 million in owners' equity, $10 million in total reserves and $100 million in loans, just like in the last example. Let's note that $1 million in owners' equity is just 1% of loans. If the bank regulators create a rule that the owners' equity must be at least 2%, it sounds very innocent, but what can the bank do to increase owners' equity? There are only two ways. First, the bank can sell additional shares of stock to increase the owners' equity. Second, the bank can reduce the amount of loans outstanding. This second option would be devastating for the economy. If the stock market is depressed and the economy is also depressed, the bank will more likely start collecting debt without making new loans then sell additional shares of stock at depressed prices. This liquidation of debt will cause the debt-deflation spiral as Irving Fisher explained. There is a third option: to raise capital by selling bonds. But this option will not help most of the banks, because most of the currency is already deposited into the banking system.

An argument can be made that selling bonds by banks is no different than selling bonds by non-financial companies, and therefore the banks should be able to raise additional capital by selling bonds.

That argument is not correct for the following reason: when a non-financial company sells bonds, the buyers of the bonds pay the company, and money moves from the bond buyers' accounts to the company's accounts. On the other hand, when a deposit institution like a bank sells bonds, and most other banks try to sell bonds, they all will be trying to stuff more green dollars into their basements, but most of the banks will not succeed because most of the green dollars are already deposited into the banking system. In addition, selling bonds would increase reserves of the bank, but it would not increase owner's equity because assets and liabilities would increase by the same amount.

As we see, any effort by regulators to increase either bank reserves or owner's equity will not be successful. The banks will have no other choice but to collect debt without making new loans. This will put in motion the debt-deflation spiral. Our economy will get started on its way to depression and devastation. The only question is, will this depression be an unintended consequence, or will it be a well-planned operation? Should we believe that Basel bankers—that is a whole bunch of international central bankers—do not know what they are doing? And is there any way to increase stability of the economy without forcing banks to stop making new loans?

Irving Fisher explained very well that liquidation of debt is the first circle in the debt-deflation spiral, which leads to economic depression. Deflation of debt necessarily must follow inflation of debt because liquidation of debt must follow accumulation of debt. It follows from Irving Fisher's debt-deflation spiral that it is this instability of money supply that causes instability of the economy, because new money is created by the banking system with the new debt, and money is destroyed when debt is liquidated.

We should assume that Basel bankers know this much. The problem is that big banks in the United States now own investment banks, which can benefit from economic depression and low prices of assets, therefore big commercial banks have incentives to knock the world economy into economic depression. Should we not assume that they will, indeed, knock the world economy into economic depression? It is very clear that the Basel agreements have been designed to stifle lending and to choke the economy into depression. In the next chapter we will discuss what should be done to keep the economy stable.

Irving Fisher was a professor of economics at Yale University, and the best economist of the 20th century. In his classic book, *Booms and Depressions* (1932, New York), Irving Fisher very clearly explained the most important factors which caused the Great Depression. He laid the foundation for the development of all the major schools of economic thought of the 20th century. Keynesian economics and monetarism have their roots in Fisher's debt-deflation spiral theory, wherein lack of aggregate demand (the backbone of Keynesian economics) and instability of money supply (the main idea of monetarism) are the two most important parts.

In 1936, almost 4 years after the publication of *Booms and Depressions*, John Maynard Keynes published his General Theory. His diagnosis? Lack of aggregate demand, with an assortment of side dishes. And the cure? To increase aggregate demand with public works financed with increased public debt.

Three decades later, in the 1960s, Milton Friedman founded the monetarist school of economic thought. He argued that the main cause of economic recessions was a fall in the money supply. That fact was, of course, one of the pillars upon which the debt-deflation spiral theory of Irving Fisher was built.

Now let's try to answer this question: Who is right, Keynesians or monetarists? We will discuss this question later in the chapter, but the short answer is that both sides are wrong. When we walk, which leg is more important, the left or the right? Our economy stands on two legs: money supply and aggregate demand, this is made very clear in Irving Fisher's theory. To argue otherwise is intellectually dishonest, even if one is awarded the Nobel Prize. If anyone deserves recognition in the field of economics, it is Irving Fisher, not those who expropriated parts of his theory and presented them as great intellectual achievements of their own. Most economists reduce their vision of economics to a set of equations and statistical research. Irving Fisher was digging much deeper into the psychological factors of economic actors, like business confidence, consumer confidence, and changes in expectations about future economic prospects that led to the Great Depression, and still are causing economic booms and busts.

Fisher's Debt-Deflation Spiral Theory has 9 factors:

1. Debt Liquidation
2. Currency Contraction
3. Dollar Growth
4. Net-Worth Reduction
5. Profit Reduction
6. Lessened Production and Trade Employment
7. Pessimism and Distrust
8. Retarded Circulation
9. Lowered Money Interest—but Raised Real Interest.

In the Preface to his book, *Booms and Depressions*, Irving Fisher wrote:

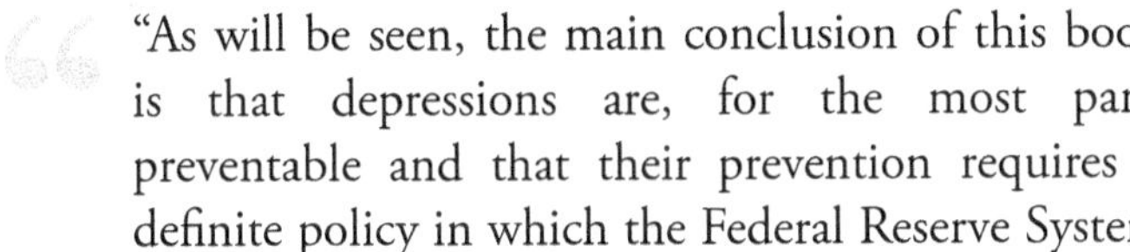

"As will be seen, the main conclusion of this book is that depressions are, for the most part, preventable and that their prevention requires a definite policy in which the Federal Reserve System must play an important role."

In the Introduction, Fisher wrote:

"How do I know there is overproduction of goods? Because more goods are for sale than the public will buy. And why, then, will the public not buy? Because they do not have the money. Why haven't they the money? Because they are not earning it. Why aren't they earning it? Because they are not producing: men and machines are idle! But if non-production is the trouble, why call it over-production?"

As we see, even in the Introduction to his book Fisher explained that demand was low because people were not working and were not earning money. The logical conclusion is to increase supply by hiring workers who will earn money and spend it to buy goods, increasing demand in the process. In other words, if I want to increase demand, I must increase supply, which is the main idea of supply-side economics. But then why is it so difficult to increase employment and to stop this vicious cycle? What is the mystery behind a depression?

The First Factor: Debt Liquidation

According to Fisher, debt is liquidated when debt is paid off. When a business or an individual borrows money from a bank, money supply increases by the amount of the loan. Let's consider the following example. Suppose, a business receives a bank loan of $100 at 10% interest. Money supply is increased—or inflated

—by $100. But new money is created with new debt. In this case, when the business pays back $110 one year later, both money supply and debt will decrease (deflate) by $110. The process of debt inflation and debt deflation has extremely profound consequences for the economy.

The Second Factor: Currency Contraction

Fisher used terms "credit currency", "deposit currency" or simply "currency" to describe money created as a result of bank lending.

When the economy is good, everyone takes out business loans to invest in existing or new businesses. This mass borrowing increases demand in the economy and also inflates the money supply as well as total debt. Money supply and debt are like two sides of the same coin. They grow together and fall together. When they grow, the economy grows. When they fall, the economy enters a downturn. It might be difficult to understand because it is so counter-intuitive, but accumulation of debt creates prosperity, and liquidation of debt causes an economic downturn.

The Third Factor: Dollar Growth

When banks collect debt but make few new loans, this mass liquidation of debt causes a sort of chain reaction. Money supply goes down—aggregate demand falls—and the general level of prices falls together with aggregate demand. The fall in the general price level is referred to as deflation. Deflation makes debt more difficult to pay, and this is why: suppose, a farmer borrowed $100 when the price of 1 bushel of corn was $2, and he could earn $100 by selling 50 bushels of corn. Suppose now, the price of corn dropped by 50%, down to $1 per bushel. Now to earn $100 the farmer needs to sell not 50 bushels of corn, but 100, which is twice as much, or a 100% increase. This means that, in nominal terms, the farmer's debt has not changed, but in real terms the farmer's debt is twice the size it was initially.

The Fourth Factor: Net-Worth Reduction

Because goods are priced in dollars, a fall in prices reduces the value of business assets (excepting cash and debts due from others), therefore a business's net worth, which is the excess of assets over liabilities, must shrink.

The Fifth Factor: Profit Reduction

Profits are the difference between the receipts and the expenses. Receipts fall when prices fall, but expenses are largely fixed. In this way, profits are reduced, and often turned into losses.

The Sixth Factor: Lessened Production, Trade, Employment

When a businessman's profits are squeezed too thin for comfort, naturally he will cut his production and lay off some of his employees, so that the community's general output, trade and employment, will slump. That is, current output coincides with current profits. Irving Fisher explained that demand and supply shrink together. When workers lose jobs, they no longer have income to spend, and it reduces aggregate demand. On the other hand, when consumers stop buying, there is no longer a need to produce as many goods as before. Supply is reduced, which leads to less production, lower employment, lower demand, and again supply is reduced, production slows, and so on, in a vicious cycle.

The Seventh Factor: Pessimism and Distrust

Irving Fisher explained that downward movements of net-worth, profits, and employment have psychological aspects. Shrinking net-worth leads to distress selling, and it implies distress. Those whose employment might be affected by a depression reduce spending in anticipation of possible loss of employment. In a word, pessimism, in a depression, becomes practically universal.

The Eighth Factor: Retarded Circulation

Fisher explained that during a depression not only a contraction, but also the slowing of currency takes place, because scared people hold on to their money a little longer—they spend it a little more slowly. If the currency contracted 50% and slowed another 50%, this means that there is only half the currency moving half as fast. Therefore, the currency as a whole will do only a quarter of its former work.

Hoarding is a slowing of currency turnover of the extreme kind. As economic depression gains strength, more and more businesses go bankrupt, and commercial banks suffer more and more losses. Many commercial banks go bankrupt themselves, wiping out depositors' life savings. As people become distrustful of commercial banks, they withdraw their money and ferret it away in stockings or under mattresses, or it ends up buried in their mother-in-law's back yard. Either way, when depositors withdraw their bills and coins, commercial banks lose their reserves against which banks make loans. As banks continue to collect debt while making very few new loans, money supply and its velocity drops further, causing more liquidation of debt, more currency contraction, and so on, down the vicious debt-deflation spiral.

The Ninth Factor: Raised Real Interest

The distinction between the money rate of interest and the real rate of interest can be explained by the following example:

Suppose, a farmer borrowed $100 for one year at 10% interest. At the time of borrowing, one bushel of corn is sold at the price of $2 per bushel, and the farmer was planning to sell ($110: $2) 55 bushels of corn to pay off his debt. Suppose now, the price of corn dropped down to $1 per bushel over the course of a year. Now the farmer needs to sell 110 bushels to pay off his debt. The farmer was planning to sell 50 bushels to pay $100 principal, and

5 bushels to pay $10 interest. Now he needs to sell 110 bushels. In effect, the farmer is paying now 50 bushels for $100 principal, and 60 bushels is his real interest.

Irving Fisher described the Great Depression very comprehensively. In 1932 he described how liquidation of debt leads to a debt-deflation spiral, and how the economic depression feeds on itself devastating millions of families and the whole economy. A reasonable observer should conclude that Irving Fisher's theory should be required reading, a mandatory part of any economic course, but for some strange reason his theory is ignored. Instead, economists ripped the heart out of his theory and debased it by presenting small parts of his theory as their own. Keynes expropriated the idea that aggregate demand is a very important part of the economy. Milton Friedman expropriated the idea that money supply is a very important part of the economy. Various other parts have been used by many other economists to create theories, without giving any credit to Irving Fisher. Worst of all, when Fisher's theory is dismembered and the vital parts are ripped out, they lose connection to other parts of the theory. When taken out of context, vital parts of Fisher's Theory are reduced to mere building blocks for new and suspect theories. For example, in Fisher's theory it is very clear that liquidation of debt leads to currency contraction and to lower demand. To argue that either low money supply (monetarism) or low demand (Keynesian) were the single main cause of the Great Depression is extremely dishonest. The science of economics needs a major, major clean-up.

A HISTORY OF ECONOMIC DEPRESSIONS

The history of economic depressions gives us an understanding of the major factors that lead to severe economic downturns. In his classic book, *Booms and Depressions* (1932, New York), Irving

Fisher provided the best explanation. He explained that liquidation of debt leads to the contraction of money in circulation, which, in turn, leads to lower demand, lower prices, lower profits, lower production, lower employment, sharp increase in bankruptcies, bank failures, and again to more liquidation of debt and so on in the vicious debt-deflation spiral, until most of the debt is either paid off or wiped out in bankruptcies.

The history of economic depressions is an essential part of American history. Let's take a quick look at the history of major economic downturns in America as described in American Passages: A History of the United States (Ayers, Gould, Oshinsky, Soderlund, 4th Ed., Cengage Advantage Books). What follows below is a concise paraphrasing.

In 1837, the largest financial panic and depression the nation had ever experienced descended on the United States. An unprecedented amount of silver poured into American banks in the mid 1830s from abroad, fueling overheated speculation. Britain's economy expanded rapidly, increasing the demand for cotton, encouraging Southern planters to buy land and slaves on credit. British investors bought up state bonds and securities, and British exporters offered generous credit to purchase a wide array of manufactured goods. American merchants, land speculators, and state governments indulged in a feast of easy credit and seemingly endless profits. Then prices for American cotton declined because of record production. The British creditors demanded repayment of loans. A major New Orleans cotton broker failed when it could not make its payments to British banks. The collapse triggered panic, desperate merchants and creditors tried to extract cash from debtors. Credit evaporated, and thousands lost jobs. Many urban families had no idea of where they would get their next meal. A second panic came in 1838, and the economy suffered until 1843. The depression began in May of 1837 after a run on the banks: customers withdrew $1 million in specie in only two days. The panic spread to every city and region of the country. The economic depression of 1837-1843 featured all major components of other economic depressions: easy credit and accumulation of debt before the panic started; a run on banks, the disappearance of credit, and the failure of businesses causing mass unemployment, after the panic started.

The American economy boomed in the mid 1850s. Not only did cotton do well, but so did the farms, factories, railroads, and cities of the North and West. The mileage of railroads tripled to more than 30,000 miles. Late in the summer of 1857, people warned that there had been too much speculation recently, that companies and individuals had borrowed too much money. The end of the Crimean War reduced demand for American farm products. When a major insurance company went under in 1857, a panic spread among New York banks, and the railroad stocks plummeted along with Western land values. Soon banks and companies across the country began to fail. Working people of all ranks lost their jobs as employers shut down the mills and factories. Across the North, hundreds of thousands of people had no income, and many were forced to rely on charity to feed and clothe themselves.

This description of the economic depression that started in 1857, contains all the major factors of any other depression. There was an economic boom financed with borrowed money, and accumulation of debt. Then there was a panic among commercial banks. It caused bank credit to dry up, which caused failure of businesses, which in turn caused both failure of commercial banks and the loss of hundreds of thousands of jobs. An interesting question is why a panic spread among New York banks after a major insurance company failed. Why would commercial banks care about the failure of an insurance company, even if it was a major one? The very short answer is that back then there was a gold standard, which means that paper money was backed by gold. Any bad news could cause a panic leading to a run on banks. Such a run is likely to leave a bank without any reserves. Bank reserves are currency against which banks make loans. When reserves are low, banks start to collect debt without making new loans, which leads to the start of a vicious debt-deflation cycle described by Irving Fisher.

In September of 1873 the banking house of Jay Cooke & Company failed. As this important bank collapsed, others followed, businesses cut back on employment, and a downturn began. The problems rivaled similar panic that had occurred in 1819, 1837, and 1857; however, the panic of 1873 was the worst of them all. The economic depression extended through the 1890s, and was then called a "Great Depression."

The Economic Depression of 1893-1897

Business had expanded during the late 1880s. In May of 1893, the weakened economy collapsed into a depression. Banks failed as depositors withdrew their funds and hoarded cash. Business activity slowed, firms cut back on production, workers were laid off. By the end of 1893, some 600 banks had failed. Court-appointed receivers ran the 119 bankrupt railroads. Another 15,000 businesses had closed. The stock market lost hundreds of millions of dollars. Most importantly, by early January 1894, 2.5 million people were unemployed. The economy was functioning at only three-quarters of its capacity. As a result, people slept on park benches, camped out in the railroad stations, and sought food at the soup kitchens.

The Great Depression

In the 1920s, the American economy was so good that economists refer to them as the Roaring Twenties. Not all segments of society shared equally in the return of good times. American farmers in the 1920s struggled with overproduction of agricultural commodities. Farmers had never benefited from the economic upturn.

Accepting the Republican Presidential nomination in 1928, Herbert Hoover proclaimed: "We in America today are nearer to the final triumph over poverty than ever before in the history of any land." It seemed that prosperity would never ever end. Then came the shocks: first, the stock market crash in October 1929, then a severe economic depression that worsened during the early 1930s. The good times of the 1920s were replaced with bread lines, soup kitchens, and the wandering homeless. The administration of President Herbert Hoover took action to relieve the crisis, but nothing seemed to work. Resentment against the President, the economic system, and the wealthy grew. The specter of social revolution arose. Pressure for political change led to the election of Franklin D. Roosevelt in 1932. By 1933, the Great Depression, as it came to be called, affected almost everyone in American society. Ever since the start of the Great Depression, economists have debated the causes of the economic instability and what should be done to prevent economic depressions from taking place.

There are many interesting questions related to the Great Depression. What, in general, causes economic instability? What were the causes of this particular economic depression? What actions should have been taken to end the Depression? And what, if anything, can we do to prevent the next depression from taking place?

Until the 1970s, when President Nixon terminated the gold standard, American dollars were backed by gold. The gold standard was the biggest source of economic instability for every country that ever used it. The reason for this is very simple. If a country imports too much in foreign goods, or imports much more than it exports, then gold moves out of the country, which creates two major problems.

First, if money leaves the country, it means that the amount of money in circulation will decrease. Since ancient times, gold was the most obvious manifestation of wealth. More than a few wars have been fought to capture cattle, slaves, and the enemy's treasury. In more modern times, imbalance in international trade provoked the introduction of tariffs, protectionism, and trade wars.

The second problem is related to the way the banking system functions. Since the 1500s banks have been using the fractional reserve method to generate loans. If 100 gold coins support loans in the amount of 500 gold coins, then 100 gold coins lost to the imbalance of international trade will reduce the amount of money in circulation by some multiple of 100 gold coins. A significant reduction of the amount of money in circulation may cause significantly lower aggregate demand, which, in turn, may start the debt-deflation spiral as described by Irving Fisher.

A monetary system based on paper money which is not backed by gold has tremendous advantages. Paper money represents claims on the wealth of the country. American dollars are claims on the wealth of the United States. Because our dollars are no longer backed by gold, we can print additional currency, which goes into circulation thus: The Fed—our central bank—prints currency (dollars). The federal government has no right to take that currency for free, otherwise the federal government would have no debt. Our Treasury prints Treasury securities and sells them to investors. From time to time the Fed buys Treasury securities and pays with printed dollars. The federal government pays interest and principal to the Fed, which can print an unlimited amount of currency to buy government debt. Now we can understand why the Great Depression lasted for so many years—the Federal Reserve could not just print billions of dollars to buy government debt because at that time, in the 1930s, we were on the gold standard. Economic instability is still possible, but now we have some tools to prevent a debt-deflation spiral from taking place.

Now let's take a look at the Great Depression as it described in American Passages, the Fourth edition.

To the average American, the economic signs during the summer of 1929 seemed encouraging. The prices of stocks traded on the New York Stock Exchange were reaching ever-higher levels. From the beginning of 1928 to September 1929 the industrial index soared from 245 to 452. The blow fell on October 29th, 1929. More than 16 million shares changed hands in a single day of panic selling. Within a few months, stock prices had lost 50% of their value.

When people lose money in financial markets, where does the lost money go? Does it disappear like light sucked into a black hole? The answer is yes, and no. Suppose, an investor bought one stock for $100, and later sold it for $50. Now one investor has $50 more, and another one has $50 less. A dollar gained by one investor is a dollar lost by someone else. Trading is a zero-sum game. Then, if the amount of money in circulation does not change, why didn't people have money during the Depression? The answer is that when the economy is in bad shape, banks continue to collect debt without making new loans. Money goes in, but nothing comes out. Commercial banks become one huge black hole. When banks act as a financial black hole, the amount of money in circulation decreases to catastrophically low levels. It causes a massive number of business failures, which, in turn, causes more bank failures because businesses default on their loans. Thousands of banks failed during the Great Depression. By 1931, 8 million people were unemployed.

It is very tempting to blame President Hoover for allowing the economic depression to gain strength, but most of the blame, in all fairness, should be assigned to the economists of the era. In the first quarter of the 20th century the classical school of economics was dominant. The classical school advocates free markets, no intervention by the government, and states that the free market will itself correct whatever is wrong with the economy. In 1932, in the midst of the Great Depression, Irving Fisher published his classic, "*Booms and Depressions,*" wherein he explained how and why the economy could stay in depression for a very long time. Still, it took about 40 years to come to the conclusion that the gold standard is not compatible with the modern economy. Back in 1930, the best action would have been to suspend the gold standard, to print paper money, and to make loans to build whatever the country needed.

Not everyone would be happy with an improved economy. At that time, many big banks owned investment banks and/or insurance companies. Investment banks and insurance companies could benefit from economic depression buying assets at very depressed prices. Big commercial banks had very powerful incentives not to make business loans, to sabotage the economy, and to make loans instead to the investment units they owned in order to buy assets pennies on the dollar. Congress recognized the fact that big commercial banks could benefit from economic depression. In 1933, Congress enacted the Glass-Steagall Act, which prohibited commercial banks from owning investment banks or insurance companies. The law was in force until 1999, when President Bill Clinton, the Fed chairman Alan Greenspan, and Congress actually repealed the Glass-Steagall Act. Now commercial banks are once again allowed to own investment units and, once again, they can benefit from economic depression and have powerful incentives to sabotage our economy. In 2008, during the financial crisis, big commercial banks bought Wall Street's biggest investment and brokerage houses. The next logical steps are: very big gains in the stock market, followed by a big crush, followed by the next Great Depression.

THE NEXT ECONOMIC DOWNTURN

In the United States, after World War II, economic downturns have taken place every ten years, plus or minus a year or two. The last downturn, often referred to as a Great Recession, started after quite a few Wall Street financial firms lost money speculating in subprime mortgages. The interesting thing is that it's not possible for everyone to lose money. If the American public—anyone except Wall Street—made money, only then would it be possible to say that one side lost money, and the other side gained as much. We know that the public lost money, and this being the case, who gained the hundreds of billions of dollars that were lost by everyone who traded, or invested in subprime mortgages? Let's take a good look at this fascinating story, because a recurrence of this might cause a second Great Depression. America must do everything possible to prevent the next economic depression, but if it does start, we need to have the tools to limit its destructive force.

As we know, there is only one situation in which money disappears, when debt is paid to a bank. Money cannot just disappear like it was sucked into some kind of a financial black hole. My spending is your saving. My loss is your gain. To understand how all parties involved could lose money, let's use a very simplified example of a market where there are two traders, A and B, and they trade two goods, goats and cows. Traders A and B are financial corporations, so any gain or loss goes to the shareholders, who are the owners. To lose money, you have to buy at a certain price and later sell at the lower price. Or buy at a certain price, and later, when the price drops, you recognize the loss by marking the price of the asset to the market price. This operation is similar to depreciation; or if you bought bonds at a certain price, and interest rates went up, the market price of your bonds went down, and you decided to keep the bonds in your accounting system at the lower market price. You have not sold the bonds, but the loss is real. Suppose now, trader A bought a goat for ten dollars, a fair market price. This was step one. Step two: trader A and B decided that the goat is not just a goat, but a small cow, so trader A sold the "small cow" to trader B at a fair market price of fifteen dollars. As a result of this successful operation, salaries, commissions, and year-end bonuses accounted for, say, three dollars out of five dollars trading profit. Step three: trader A and B decided that this small cow is actually a big cow, so trader B sold the "big cow" to Trader A at a fair market price of twenty dollars, making five dollars profit. The party now is in Trader B's house. Step four: everyone recognized that the big cow has shrunk into a small goat, so trader A marked the price of the "cow" down to a market price of a goat. Let's count the beans. Trader A made a profit of $5 and a loss of $10 when he marked the price down. Trader B made $5 profit, which equals a $5 overall loss of trader A. In this very simplified example profits equal losses, both from trading. The only way for everyone to suffer losses is to either buy an overpriced goat from the beginning and then mark it down to $5, or to pay excessive commissions and bonuses to the traders, or some combination of both. It means that subprime mortgage securities were overpriced from the beginning, the equivalent of a $5 goat to be sold to trader A at the beginning by someone who was not trader B. We know that mortgages originate in the banking system, and whoever sold the overpriced mortgages to the Wall Street's brokerage houses should have known that it would bankrupt them. Incidentally or by design, big banks ended buying the bankrupt brokerage houses.

At the time of this writing, in the summer of 2018, speculation in stocks is rampant. An interesting question is whether it is possible for everyone to lose money trading stocks. With creative accounting, it should be possible. Markets of speculative goods have psychology that is very different from market psychology of ordinary goods. When the prices of ordinary goods go up, demand falls, and prices go down. When the price of speculative goods goes up, smart speculators jump in early and get out early. Dumb speculators jump on the bandwagon and drive the very last increase of demand and prices. As demand weakens, prices collapse. The question is how badly the collapse of the stock market will damage the economy. Irving Fisher identified the stock market crash as the very first event that greatly increased the sense of economic insecurity. At that time, in 1929, only a few percent of Americans were investing in the stock market, and when they lost money, the damaging effect on the economy was tremendous. At the present time a much larger percentage of American families own stocks, and the damaging effect on the economy will be correspondingly larger.

What can be done to limit excessive speculation on the part of uninformed Americans? First of all, we need to reduce incentives to manipulate market prices of stocks. Prices can be manipulated in a number of ways. When you hear a radio advertisement telling you that J.P. Morgan bank has accumulated a million ounces of silver, and that price of silver will go up, what does it mean? It means that Wall Street sharks accumulate assets at low prices, and unload them to the public when they are done buying. If J.P. Morgan is no longer buying, then it is time to sell, and not to buy. The first thing that should be done is to enact a law requiring a handful of the biggest financial institutions to report their assets and trading positions every month. For example, J.P. Morgan would be required to report how much silver it owns, how much silver it is going to buy and sell (futures contracts), and options on futures contracts. Will it end these dirty games? No. The public will be able to see the dynamic of J.P. Morgan's position for a number of months, but there will still be a cat and mouse game. Say, J.P. Morgan is buying one ton of silver over the next three months. Does it mean that they are still in accumulation mode? The public might start increasing purchases of silver, and the bank might unload two tons of silver over those three months to the public. The bank's sale of one ton of silver might scare the public into selling three tons of silver at low prices, and the bank will be only too happy to buy it at the low price. Still, even this game will give the public a better chance to understand what is going on over a long period of time. As it stands now, the public has no chance against Wall Street.

The second thing to do would be to prohibit exotic derivatives. Even put and call options on futures contracts are not really needed, and their liquidation, or prohibition, would greatly simplify the financial game. Wall Street, at the present time, is a financial casino. Americans save money and make investments, but the role of most of Wall Street's firms is to separate people from their money. Only Venture Capital firms make money by providing a very useful service: giving start-up capital to new companies, but even they played a destructive role in the dotcom financial mania of the 1990s. The rest of the financial system simply has no scruples. Some years ago, they even lobbied to privatize the Social Security system. The problem with that idea is that nothing would prevent private companies that make investments for the privatized Social Security system to buy "goats" at inflated prices, by a dumb mistake or by smart and evil intent. If billions of dollars are easy to steal, they will be stolen. Should we really believe that people who attended the best business schools money could buy could not distinguish between

AAA rated investments and financial junk? The fact that some corrupted insurance company insures you from the junk related losses does not turn junk into gold. Those who work in corrupt firms have the opportunity to make really good money by bankrupting the firm and creating losses for the shareholders. But the bigger problem is that troubling news in the financial system might cause an avalanche effect where the weakest businesses go bankrupt first, increasing the unemployment rate and the sense of financial insecurity, and the wall of engulfing snow pushes down more secure parts of the economy. With our history of economic downturns every ten years or so, we should not assume that the year 2020 will be any different. Politicians will claim the dumb economic policy of President Trump caused an increase in government debt and now chickens are coming home to roost, but the simple truth is that government debt is not any worse that private debt, and liquidation of any debt will necessarily reduce both money supply and aggregate demand in the economy; and if they drop significantly, it, without any doubt, will cause an economic downturn. If a mild economic downturn is allowed to feed on itself, then a potentially dangerous situation will become a deadly one, so the question becomes how to maintain steady money supply (if you are a monetarist), or how to maintain steady aggregate demand (if you are a Keynesian).

Irving Fisher explained that several factors might be working at the same time to push the economy into an economic depression. Any bad news in the economy increases economic insecurity. Workers start worrying about their jobs. They cut spending in order to save some money for a rainy day. Lower spending means lower demand in the economy. Unsold goods accumulate in the warehouses. Manufacturers cut production and lay off workers. Laid-off workers now don't have any income to spend. This means more bad news and the start of the next cycle: lower spending, lower prices, lower production, and more layoffs. Still more bad news, still lower spending, and so on. The economy is in a tailspin, moving lower and lower in circles down the vicious spiral of economic destruction, but this is only one half of the picture. The other half of the picture describes what is happening in the financial system. There is its own downward spiral which interacts with the spiral of the wider economy, and both comprise a single spiral of economic destruction. Let's take a look.

As we know, commercial banks use the fractional reserve principle in their operations. "You want a loan? Here is your checkbook, and we just transferred a million dollars to your account." That is it. The bank just "printed" a million bucks without even using a printing press, ink and paper. Now you can spend your money by writing checks, which are not money, but are instruments to give your money to anyone you wish. Because people use checks, credit cards, and debit cards, the real green dollars stay somewhere in the basement of the bank most of the time. Those green dollars in the "basement" are no longer considered to be money, because they are no longer circulating outside in the economy. Those real green dollars are bank reserves to be given to customers when they withdraw money in cash from their accounts. The American banking system was, in principle, the same even a hundred years ago.

The banking system was inherently unstable. If there were, say, ten million dollars in deposits generated against only one million of real green dollars in reserves, and customers want to withdraw all the money from their accounts in cash, how much cash would they get? Only one million. It is called a run on the bank, and any bank that cannot satisfy reasonable requests to withdraw money in cash is technically bankrupt. Here I have to make one controversial comment. The only way to make a banking system really strong is the following: imagine for one minute that people don't have money to make primary deposits. It means that all banking reserves are the bank's own capital, and no one can withdraw the reserves. And those who have deposits/loans cannot really demand large sums to withdraw in cash, because the bank might "call" the loan, which means to close the loan account and demand all the debt to be paid back immediately. The point is that the more monetary savings people have, the more primary deposits they will have, and the more unstable the banking system will become.

Suppose now, customers decided to withdraw only one million dollars out of ten million in deposits. Then the banking system is left without reserves. This means that banks must not only stop making new loans, but they have to cancel one million dollars in existing loans, wiping out ten percent of the money supply and aggregate demand. If both drop by ten percent, it means the start of an economic depression. Customers whose loans are canceled must sell their assets in order to pay back the bank loans. The widespread selling is pushing prices down as this sudden increase in supply is much larger than demand. Now, what happens when the prices go down? A business was paying, say, $10 for raw materials and labor, and was selling the manufactured goods for eleven dollars, making one-dollar profit. If the price suddenly dropped by ten percent, then all the profit is wiped out, business firms start either cutting production or closing businesses completely. As workers are laid off, spending drops together with demand and prices, starting another vicious spiral in the non-financial sector of the economy. As we see, a very mild run on banks can have horrific consequences for the whole economy. As banks started to cancel loans without making new loans, money supply and aggregate demand dropped, pushing prices farther down and forcing more businesses to cut production, lay off workers, or go bankrupt. As more businesses became bankrupt, financial losses in the banking system increased, and banks themselves started to go bankrupt. At that time there was no insurance for bank deposits, and primary depositors were losing their life savings. They started to withdraw their deposits in cash. This hoarding of cash by the public forced the bank to cancel more and more loans in order to satisfy withdrawal requests by primary depositors. As Fisher writes, banks started to raid depositors who were trying to raid banks. Mutual raiding, so to speak. As banks canceled deposits of the borrowers and called in more loans, this raid on depositors started the next circle of pushing down both money supply and aggregate demand, causing still lower prices, lower spending, and so on. As the non-financial sector of the economy was getting worse, increased bankruptcies worsened the situation in the financial sector as well, forcing the banks to raid more borrowers and cancel their loans, causing still worse economic conditions in the non-financial sector, which in turn were causing a still worse situation in the financial sector, and so on down the spiral of mutually assured economic destruction.

Now let's take a quick look at a few schools of economic thought in order to find out what they offer in general, and what they suggest we do if and when the economic downturn picks up its destructive speed.

In the 1970s, Robert Lucas, an economist at the University of Chicago, created rational expectations school of economic thought. He argued the following: when people start hoarding cash, cutting spending and reducing both money supply and aggregate demand, then both prices and wages will drop, the purchasing power of money will increase, and there will be no need for any government action to increase the money supply and aggregate demand.

Thus far, this is an old argument from classical economics—that the economy can always heal itself, and any government intervention will only cause more harm. But Lucas added a new argument to the old one. He claimed that any predictable monetary policy would be ineffective because if everyone knows that the Federal Reserve will increase the money supply every time the unemployment rate goes up, then business firms will build that typical policy into their expectations and increase their prices accordingly. The logic here is that firms always act rationally to protect their interests, and a predictable monetary policy cannot fool them. This is where the name of rational expectation comes from. The theory, in effect, states that any attempt to increase money supply and aggregate demand will only increase prices without increasing the economic output.

There are at least a handful of logical mistakes in the rational expectations theory, and we need to identify them so that at the start of the next economic downturn they can be avoided.

1. The old idea from classical economics: when money supply and aggregate demand drop, then wages and prices will drop also rather quickly. This idea has long been outdated. Irving Fisher wrote that when there is an inflation in prices, workers are very quick to ask for higher wages to compensate for lower purchasing power of money. But when there is deflation, then prices drop, and the business profits drop also, but workers usually somehow don't understand that deflation did, indeed, increase the purchasing power of money, and they are always very reluctant to accept lower wages. Wages, in the jargon of economists, are very "sticky" to the downside, and that is why deflation always drives weak firms into bankruptcy. It is very important to remember that deflation kills off the weak.

2. The second idea from classical economics: when prices drop (deflation), the purchasing power of money will increase, and there will be no need for any government action to increase the money supply and aggregate demand. False. Irving Fisher explained that deflation increases the real debt, or the size of debt

in real terms. For example, a farmer borrowed $2 when the price of one bushel of wheat was $2, so he owes one bushel of wheat in his mind. Now, if the price of wheat dropped to $1 per bushel, the farmer has to sell two bushels in order to pay his $2 debt. Deflation makes every dollar bigger, Fisher wrote, and makes debt larger in real terms, and more difficult to pay. This is the second reason why deflation kills off the weak firms, and this is also important to remember, because when the weakest firms start laying off workers or go bankrupt, this bad economic news is exactly what causes lower spending, lower demand, and so on in circles down the spiral of economic destruction—and the need for someone, anyone, to increase the money supply and aggregate demand.

3. Lucas claimed the following: If everyone knows that the Federal Reserve will increase the money supply when the unemployment rate goes up, then firms, being rational, will simply increase their prices, and the monetary expansion will only cause higher prices without higher output. False. Two points here.

First, the Federal Reserve cannot directly increase the money supply unless the Fed makes a loan directly to the government, or buys something valuable—like gold—directly from a seller who is not a bank. The Fed is usually buying Treasury securities from commercial banks, and it increases the reserves of the selling bank. But reserves are not money, as we know. Only when the bank makes a loan against those reserves, the money supply increases by the amount of the new loan. Bluntly speaking, a bank may sell Treasuries to the Fed, accept the payment as an increase of its account in the Fed, and then choose to sit on that account and not to make new loans. Or the bank might even take cash—real green dollars—as payment for the sold Treasuries, put the cash in the basement, increasing its reserves, and then sit on those reserves without making new loans. In short, the fact that the Fed is injecting reserves into the banking system does not mean that the Fed is increasing the money supply, aggregate demand, and prices in the economy. If there is widespread hoarding of money, banks will need those reserves to meet the customer's request to withdraw cash from their accounts.

Secondly, when unemployment goes up, and the Fed is trying to inject more reserves into the banking system, this is troubling. Higher unemployment is the kind of news that increases the sense of economic insecurity and can cause lower spending and lower money supply as people lose confidence and stop taking out new loans, lower demand, lower prices (deflation), and so on in circles down the spiral of economic destruction. In such a debt-deflation spiral the problem is deflation, and not inflation. Why would any rational person who has taken at least an introductory course in economics in college make such a self-defeating decision to raise prices?

4. A few pages back we were discussing how the two spirals of economic devastation—one in the financial system, and the second one in the "real economy"—were interacting to form a single vicious spiral of economic destruction. When a bank calls in a loan, both money supply and aggregate demand will fall. If customers don't have confidence to take out new loans, they will pay off the old loans, and both money supply and aggregate demand will fall the same way, just as if the bank called in the loan. Which side is more guilty? Fisher writes that both sides were raiding each other, causing liquidation of debt in the debt-deflation spiral. In such a situation, where the main threat is both deflation of debt in the banking system and general deflation of prices in the "real economy," a limited increase in the general level of prices would only bring prices to the level they were at before deflation, and it would be very positive for the economy. Because low demand causes deflation, and low prices, in turn, cause lower production, lower prices cause lower supply. In such a situation,

moderately higher prices would encourage production and increase output. Lucas claimed that even during an economic recession a monetary expansion affects only prices, not output. Let's consider a simple example. Suppose the main goal of the monetary expansion is to increase output, namely, the supply of housing. The banks are obligated to make loans only to build housing, but not loans to buy the existing ones. Output will increase. Suppose now, during an economic depression when demand is very low, the banks are obligated to make loans only to buy houses, but not to build them. The result will be that demand and prices will increase, and higher prices will make construction of houses more profitable, which will encourage construction of houses, which means more output. This reasoning, that during an economic depression aggregate demand is the most important factor is, of course, Keynesian. In Irving Fisher's theory of the debt-deflation spiral the aggregate demand is also one of the most important factors. Any way you look at the rational expectations theory it, in the short run, fooled a lot of people, but in the long run is surely dead.

Why have we discussed the rational expectations theory first, before any other major theory? Because this theory is the worst of them all. Now we will take a look at the second worst of all major theories, monetarism.

MONETARISM

Milton Friedman claimed that a Keynesian policy to stimulate the economy would be harmful. He argued that most economic recessions occurred not because of lower spending, but because of a fall in the quantity of money in circulation, and he offered a simple solution: to keep the money supply steady. Let's examine this point before we move on to the next one. After reading the text above anyone should understand that the money supply drops when people cut their spending, pay off any debt they owe to banks, and try to save more money. People do these things because they are concerned about the slowing economy, which is caused by, or is the result of, slowing bank credit. To keep money supply steady would require a very strict government control which Friedman very much disliked. Friedman selected a small part of Irving Fisher's debt-deflation theory, which is all about liquidation of debt and a fall in money supply, appropriated it without even mentioning Fisher's name, and proposed to keep the money supply steady. But if the money supply and the aggregate demand could be easily kept steady, we would not be discussing the next economic downturn.

Now let's try to create a chain of events that typically lead to an economic downturn. But where to start? Is this chain a circle or a spiral? Let's start at the end of the last downturn, when both the financial sector and the "real economy" had already finished exchanging devastating blows. Most of the weakest firms in the economy and the weakest banks in the financial sector were already bankrupt, and the worst of the bad news, like raiding each other, was behind us. Irving Fisher's theory can be summarized in just a few steps. Step 1: Banks start making loans again. Step 2: The economy improves. Step 3: Banks reach their limits to make new loans, and it marks the highest point of the economic expansion. Step 4: Banks start to collect debt in an amount higher than they expend in new loans, and the economy enters a downturn. Step 5: Liquidation of debt will push the economy to the lowest point of the downturn, where most of the debt that banks want to collect is already collected. This marks the end of the business cycle, and the economy is positioned to grow again. The essence of the whole story can be summarized in one sentence: accumulation of debt leads to economic prosperity; liquidation of debt leads to an economic downturn. Fisher wrote that liquidation of debt is not possible without accumulating the debt in the economy in the first place.

Let's go back to Friedman's proposal. He accused the Fed of failing to inject cash into the economy in order to keep the money supply steady, but here is the problem with his argument. The Fed is not Santa Claus bearing gifts. The Fed could only buy something valuable from banks or other private parties—gold and other precious metals, or the government securities, or even private debt ranging from bonds of respected companies down to the lowliest subprime mortgages—at the right prices. But at that time our monetary system was based on the gold standard, and the Fed did not have a legal right to print currency that was not backed by gold. Friedman's accusation is total and complete nonsense.

The only thing that would have improved the economy for sure would have been to abandon the gold standard. Then, and only then, would the Fed have had the legal right to print currency not backed by gold and to start buying assets, injecting cash into the economy. Would this have been inflationary? No. In the short run it would stop or at least reduce the speed at which the money supply was falling. In the long run the money supply would not even increase. Why? Because it is a loan, and not a gift. Suppose the Fed printed $100 and bought a bond of a reputable company for $100. Money supply increased by $100, if the Fed bought the bond straight from the company. Over some time, the company paid back $100 plus $10 in interest, so, in the long run, money supply decreased by $110, which means net reduction of the money supply by $10.

There is another problem with Friedman's argument. When the Fed buys something—anything—from a commercial bank, the Fed increases the bank's reserves. Now it is up to the bank whether it wants to make loans against the increased reserves. So,

Friedman's diagnosis was wrong. The Fed could only increase the reserves of the banking system, and only after abandoning the gold standard system. Unfortunately, abandoning the gold standard system was unimaginable at that time, as the paper money was a claim on gold, and not on the wealth of the country. Neither Irving Fisher nor Keynes proposed abandoning the gold standard.

As we see, the Fed could not keep the money supply steady for two reasons. First, it could not print currency that was not backed by gold. At that time paper money was like a warehouse receipt serving as evidence that you own some gold, and the gold was real money. The second reason is that when the debt-deflation spiral picks up speed, and when both the financial system and the "real economy" are raiding each other, banks need much more reserves in order to meet withdrawal requests. Only a massive injection of reserves into the banking system could have improved the situation, but the Fed did not have a right to print the currency not backed by gold.

Milton Friedman has misled us by concentrating our attention on the fall in the money supply, which the Fed could not possibly cure. An increase in the money supply will of course increase the aggregate demand, but for that to happen banks must be willing to make new loans, and the "real economy" must be willing to take on additional debt. On the other hand, when the economy becomes worse, neither are banks willing to make new loans, nor is the "real economy" willing to take on additional debt. And then lower money supply will push down the aggregate demand, and lower aggregate demand will make the economy worse, and so on in circles down the debt-deflation spiral. To argue that the fall in the money supply was the main factor leading to the Great Depression, and the Fed was responsible for is both false and dishonest.

But this was only the first time Milton Friedman misled us. Let's take a look at the second: He explained that monetary policy works with "long and variable lags." When the economy enters a downturn, the Fed usually starts purchasing Treasures, the government's debt (fortunately, President Nixon's Administration took our monetary system off the gold standard, and the Fed can print as much currency as is needed). The Fed, as a result, will have more Treasuries on its balance sheet, and the banks will have more money (reserves) in their accounts in the Fed. Friedman claimed that the Fed is always late to recognize that a new downturn is taking place in the economy. In addition, monetary policy is always slow to affect the real economy. The result, he claimed, was that the Fed was making a good economy excessively overheated, and after that, when trying to correct course, the Fed would make a bad economy even worse. What a bucket of a story! But can this bucket hold the water? No, there are a couple of big holes in it.

Friedman claimed that since the Fed only makes things worse, it should abandon any active monetary policy, and adopt a policy of steady but moderate increases in the money supply at a rate consistent with stable prices and long-term economic growth.

Friedman's argument brings to mind a picture of a car fishtailing on a slippery road. As the driver makes an effort to correct the course, they over-correct, and the car fishtails, veering in the opposite direction and so on until the car runs off the road and hopefully into a soft object. This picture has a certain emotional appeal, but the solution is equivalent to abandoning any effort at steering. Let's recall that Friedman did claim that the Fed failed to steer the economy in the right direction, and it allegedly caused the Great Depression. Was the economy fishtailing before the Great Depression? No. During the "Roaring Twenties" the economy showed steady growth for a decade. The weather was sunny, the snow was soft and white, people did not pay attention to the fact that somewhere high in the mountains the snow was accumulating dangerously, and eventually it caused an avalanche. Liquidation of debt.

Now let's leave metaphor behind and try to figure out a few important things. First, why were classical economists against any government intervention? Why did they not support government regulation to keep the money supply increasing steadily at a reasonably low rate? The first reason we can think of is, if gold is money then money can be dug out of the ground, increasing the monetary base wherever the gold mines exist. Also, the international trade allowed British merchants to exchange locally manufactured goods for gold in other countries increasing the monetary base.

The second reason: when gold is deposited into a bank, it becomes reserves against which the bank can generate loans. Imagine now that the banking system was increasing the money supply for, say, ten years. At the beginning banks were keeping one real gold coin in reserves to support three gold coins loaned. Gradually, it became one coin against four coins loaned, and finally one coin in reserves against five in loans and deposits. If the bank reserves did not change, then an increase from 1:3 to 1:5 means an increase in money supply by 66%. In this scenario for prices to stay steady, the supply of goods also must increase by the same percentage, and the velocity of money remains unchanged.

The only reliable way to keep money supply steady would have been a radical reform of the banking system, and abandoning the gold standard. Friedman claimed that a steady but reasonably low increase in the money supply would allow the economy to become more stable, but that argument was misleading, not so much in what he said, but in what he did not say. He did not tell us that the Fed can only print currency (after the Nixon administration abandoned the gold standard), buy gold, Treasuries, or even subprime mortgages, and it would increase the reserves in the banking system, but it is up to the bank managers to decide whether to make loans or just to sit on those reserves: the Fed cannot control the money supply and keep it steady.

During the Great Depression the problem was the gold standard. Today we no longer have that problem, but we do have another one: the top management of big banks. We'll go into that more a little later. Why is it important? Because if we are misled by this doctrine of monetarism and develop a false sense of security, and believe that the Fed does, indeed, control the money supply, then the next economic downturn may start as a very mild one but turn into an economic depression. Still worse, Milton Friedman claimed that any active monetary policy beyond maintaining a steady but moderate increase in the money supply would be actually harmful. Let's take a look at a related story.

This story is about the trade-off between unemployment and inflation, the Phillips curve. In 1959, British economist A.W. Phillips, discovered an apparent correlation between the unemployment rate and the rate of change of wages. These two rates move in the opposite directions, with wages sharply accelerating upward when the unemployment rate is low at about 4 percent. This happens because when unemployment is low, then employers are willing to pay higher wages. Since wages are a large part of production costs, higher wages increase prices of goods and services, which means inflation. Phillips constructed a curve showing the relationship between unemployment and inflation. During the 1960s, there was an apparent trade-off between unemployment and inflation, but in the second half of the decade the inflation rate started to accelerate and went ballistic—almost straight up—as unemployment went down only slightly. From 1966 to 1969 the inflation rate doubled, going from 3% to 6%, while the unemployment rate dropped only one half of one percent.

Before we continue the story, let's try to figure out what was going on and why. The unemployment rate is always more sticky at low values. In other words, it hesitates to go down. We can identify at least two reasons. First, no matter how good the economy is, there will always be people who are looking for their first jobs after leaving high school, college, military service, etc. Second, we can argue that a good economy might even increase unemployment. Why? Because when the economy is slow, then people sit tight and don't move. When the economy improves, many people quit their jobs and start looking for better ones. The result is that even if there are millions of jobs available, the unemployment rate will not go lower then about 3%.

Now let's try to answer the following question. During the 1960s, there was an apparent trade-off between unemployment and inflation. During the 1970s, that trade -off fell apart, and the economy managed to have both high unemployment and high inflation. Why did it happen?

The Phillips Curve has a very simple explanation. When unemployment is low, employers are willing to pay higher wages, which means higher labor costs. Higher costs of production are passed on to the consumer who pays higher prices, which means higher inflation. In the second half of the 1960s the Vietnam war was the main cause of higher inflation. It was also the time of the civil rights movement, and demands for higher wages were a part of it. Higher wages caused higher prices, which caused demands for still higher wages, and so on up the inflationary spiral. It was a cost-push inflation, and it was not a monetary phenomenon, contrary to what monetarists say. Usually, when unemployment goes up, inflation goes down.

In 1968, Friedman claimed that firms and workers were fooled by inflation, and predicted that inflation would persist even in the face of high unemployment. It was logical. He encouraged workers not to be fools and to demand higher wages, which caused higher prices. Friedman put in motion the inflationary spiral. The logical result was the inflationary spiral to continue moving higher, and high unemployment throughout the 1970s. The Phillips Curve fell apart. Because employers paid too high wages, and they did not have money to invest, since profits were too low. The result was high inflation and high unemployment. Only in 1979-1982 inflation was put under control when the Fed crashed the economy with very tight monetary policy.

Now, back to Friedman's bucket of stories. His next story, which is related to the Phillips curve, is the third instance in which he misled us. His logic goes as follows: if we were to double the money supply, but also to double all prices and wages, the unemployment rate would not change. Was he right? Yes, but with a qualification. We'd have to double everything instantly, or overnight. If I could double the money supply, asked Friedman, without any real effects, then why would an increase in the money supply by the Federal Reserve have any real effect? Let's answer his question before we go to his answer. If everything, including all kinds of income and all kinds of expenses, were to double, in practical sense nothing has changed. Now let's take a look at what happens when the Fed tries to increase the money supply gradually.

When the Fed tries to increase the money supply, it buys something valuable on the open market, most often Treasury securities. Banks sell the Treasuries in return for an increase in their accounts in the Fed. If the bank managers decide to make loans against the increased reserves, the money supply will increase.

If new loans are made to increase demand—for example, to BUY apartments, houses, and chicken farms—this increase of the money supply will increase demand and prices, but will not create many jobs, and will not affect unemployment much. If the new loans are made to increase aggregate supply—to BUILD new houses and chicken farms—this increase in the money supply will increase aggregate demand (to pay for construction materials and labor), aggregate supply (when the new houses and chicken farms have been built and placed on the market for sale), will create many jobs, and will affect the unemployment rate. It will also increase the economic output and will create wealth.

As we see, an increase in the money supply by making new loans to create new wealth (to BUILD new houses, etc.) will create jobs and will affect the unemployment rate, while new loans to BUY old stuff—or even new stuff—will be pushing up only aggregate demand and prices, which means inflation. That is why Friedman misled us by offering a false choice: "If I were to double the money supply, but also to double all prices and wages, what would happen to the unemployment rate?" No, you can't double the money supply, prices, and wages, without any real effects on the economy! That is just a cheap shot, like throwing trash into a Keynesian garden in the middle of the night and hoping that no one will notice. In the real-world money supply is increased not by doubling all related statistics, but by making loans to increase not only demand and prices (implying harmful inflation), but also economic output, aggregate supply, and to create productive jobs.

Loans to CREATE new wealth will increase many good things. Loans to BUY existing wealth will be pushing demand and prices upward, with three possible outcomes: very good, good, and bad. If the economy is in a debt-deflation spiral, then loans to buy provide some support to arrest deflation, which is very good. In an overheated economy loans to buy will further increase harmful inflation, which is bad. In a normal economy with steady prices loans to buy existing wealth are still needed. You cannot buy your dream home without a mortgage loan.

Now, with a better understanding of the general picture, let's try to answer Friedman's question, the second one in his story. "How can it be," asked Friedman, "that I could double the money supply without any real effects, but an increase in the money supply by the Federal Reserve has real effects? Why is it that a 5% increase in the money supply does not immediately raise prices by 5%, but instead raises prices by only a little and leads to a rise in output instead?" Let's repeat again that Friedman could not double the money supply without any real effects, except in his imagination, but an increase in the bank reserves (not the money supply) by the Federal Reserve does have real effects as the bank managers will make some productive loans against those reserves.

Now the second part of his question: why is it that a 5% increase in the money supply does not immediately raise prices by 5%, but instead raises prices by only a little and leads to a rise in output instead? The answer to this question requires explanation. We need to recall the mechanism by which the banks can generate, say, $10 in loans/deposit against only $1 in reserves. The main factor is that most bank customers accept loans in the form of a deposit in the bank's accounting system, and new money can be created with only a pen, paper, a promise to pay back the borrowed money plus interest, and some reserves (real green dollars). Customers write checks to each other, the accounting system moves money (numbers on created deposits), but the real green dollars rarely leave the basement. The easiest way to create new loans/deposits would be in a banking system in which only a single monopoly bank exists, because there would be no other bank to send money to. Now let's start a new banking system with bank A who has a customer (A), and bank B who has another customer (B). Bank A started operations with

$100 in reserves, and bank B also started with $100 in reserves. Suppose now, customer A took out a $10 loan from his bank, and customer B took out a $10 loan from his bank. $20 of new money was created. Now, one customer A bought something from customer B and wrote a $10 check to him. This check will move $10 from bank A to bank B. Now, one customer B bought something from customer A and wrote a $10 check, which will move $10 from bank B to bank A. When payments are made, nothing, or no real green dollars, move from one bank to another, because these two checks canceled each other out. But loans have been made, new money has been created, payments have been made, and real green dollars are still in the basement of the two banks. The point here is that IT TAKES SOME TIME to increase the money supply with new loans and new debt. That is why if a bank sells Treasuries, etc., it will increase the bank's reserves, but money supply will increase only after customers take out loans. This increase in money supply will push up aggregate demand and prices only after the customers start spending the new money created with their new loans, new deposits and new debt. Loans and debt are almost the same thing except you pay back the loan plus interest.

Now back to Friedman's question. A 5% increase in the money supply will not immediately raise prices by 5% because the new money is not immediately spent. Instead, it raises prices by only a little and leads to a rise in output, because some of the new money supply will go into loans to create new wealth—new houses and chicken farms, for example. As we have seen earlier, loans to BUY existing wealth do not increase economic output, but loans to CREATE new wealth do.

Now, for a final example. A mortgage loan to buy a house—old or new—will create only one short job for a real estate agent, but a construction loan to build a new house will create a number of jobs in construction and construction materials industries. If the cost of construction is, say, $300,000 (materials and labor, not counting price of land), $30,000 per year in wages, it will create ($300 divide by $30) ten jobs for one year, and it will increase economic output by $300,000. So, in the real world, an increase of the money supply by making new loans takes some time; and then it takes some time to spend the borrowed money (for example, a construction manager will be spending $300,000 of his construction budget over the whole period of construction, which might take years). That is why a new $300,000 construction loan will immediately increase the money supply by $300,000; but prices and wages will be affected slowly because the spending of the borrowed money is slow. Instead, this $300,000 construction loan will increase the economic output. Granted, loans to BUY (mortgage loans) will affect the aggregate demand and prices much more quickly than loans to CREATE new wealth.

Let's see what Friedman told us about why a 5% increase in the money supply will not immediately raise prices by 5%, but instead raises prices only a little and leads to output instead (just like in our construction example above). Friedman told us that a 5% increase in the money supply does not immediately raise prices by 5%, and leads instead to a rise in output because—get this! —firms and workers are FOOLED. Workers demanded too little in wages because they underestimated the coming rate of inflation, and firms set their prices too low because they underestimated the coming rise in their wage and supplier costs. The result is that a 5% rise in the money supply raises prices much less than 5%, and leads to a rise in output instead.

Alright, let's take a closer look at Friedman's assumptions. The first assumption is that workers demanded too little because they underestimate the coming rate of inflation. Let's stop and think here. First, in a free market wages are supposed to be set by the market, and not by the demands of the workers. Why was a free-marketeer (Friedman) telling the world that workers were demanding too little, and encouraging them to increase their demands, in effect starting wage and price increases that grow into an inflationary spiral? An inflationary spiral is just the opposite of the debt-deflation spiral. In effect, Friedman advised workers to start the inflationary spiral wherein higher wages lead to higher prices; which cause still more demands for higher wages to compensate for the loss of purchasing power; which increase labor costs and lead to still higher prices... and so on and so forth. Was Friedman so dense as to not to understand it? No! He actually predicted that workers and firms would start to build expected inflation rates into their wages demands and prices, and the Phillips curve would disappear. In other words, inflation would persist even in the face of high unemployment.

He was right, of course. If you pay an arsonist to burn down a house tomorrow, then today you can predict that tomorrow a house will go up in flames. In effect, Friedman paid an "arsonist," and predicted the outcome. In the 1970s the Phillips curve fell apart; the economy was having both high unemployment and high inflation. Friedman managed to mislead everyone (except Keynesians), including the Nobel Prize committee who awarded him the Nobel Prize.

This is a serious accusation, so let's double and triple-check our logic, which is, in a nutshell, simple enough. The increased money supply can raise either mostly prices, or it can raise mostly production and output. When the economy is normal, and prices and wages are stable, then unemployment and inflation have a relationship just like in the Phillips curve. You reduce unemployment by one percent, and you will get an increase in inflation by about one percent, because workers start looking for greener pastures, and higher wages get reflected in higher prices, which means inflation.

Notice also that lower unemployment means more workers building houses and chicken farms, which means higher aggregate supply and lower prices. Now, where does the money for wages come from? Money can come from two main sources: the firm's income and bank loans. Officially, the firm will always say that a bank loan is needed for investment, but the truth is that higher wages leave less money for investment, so the fact is that increase in the money supply might go to finance higher wages and not investment.

There are two kinds of inflation. First example: average wages were $10 per hour, and a basket of goods and services was also priced at $10. As a result of inflation, the price of the basket increased to $20, but wages remained the same, so now workers need to work two hours instead of one hour to buy one basket of goods. Why does this happen? Low supply is the usual suspect. If billions of chickens suddenly die in the United States from some poultry epidemic, then you can bet the price for chicken will increase. If there is a nuclear war, and the country is producing ten times less than it was consuming before the war, how much of an increase in wages should the workers demand in order to increase their consumption to the old level? Firms might take out bank loans to finance higher wages, but can the country eat ten chickens if it is raising only one? The point here is that workers demanding and getting higher wages will not increase their consumption, so workers will get only higher wages and higher prices.

The second example of inflation of a different kind. Wages are $10 per hour, and the basket of goods is also priced at $10. The government started a program to print money, but only for investment (to build houses and chicken farms). If there is an economic depression and millions of unemployed workers, it might be necessary to print a lot of money. The price of a basket of goods might increase to $20, just like in the first example. Why? Because of a sharp increase in money supply. But, unlike in the first example, now there is higher output. How many baskets will the country consume or save? The more we produce, the more we consume or save, regardless of the price of the basket. You can play with lines of supply, demand, consumption, production, and anything else, but this statement will always be true. During the depression unsold goods will represent savings, but it will have an unwanted effect. In a normal economy, workers cannot increase their consumption by demanding higher wages. Unless, of course, at the cost of lower investment as firms are very likely to reduce it in the face of higher wage demands while increasing prices to generate income to meet higher wage demands.

Understanding how wage and price spirals develop and pick up the speed, let's take another look at Friedman's story: "workers set their wage demands too low, because they underestimate the coming rate of inflation." What is the logic here? It is, pretty clearly, that workers should demand higher wages. The result, logically, will be a combination of lower investment and higher inflation as the wage and price spiral develops and picks up the speed.

Friedman implied that a 5% increase in the money supply would necessarily increase inflation, and it would harm workers. Was he right? Suppose the Fed printed billions of dollars and made a loan to Amazon Corporation which decided to build modern new cities with very large city blocks, so that inside every residential city block there will be an Amazon shopping center. When the loan was made, the money supply increased by 5%. A couple of years later construction has been completed, apartments have been sold, and Amazon paid back the loan plus interest. Two years construction loan at 5% interest per year is around 10%, so Amazon will pay back an amount that is 10% larger than the amount borrowed. It means that the money supply will be reduced by an amount that is 10% larger than the original loan. Both the supply of housing and economic output increased, and the money supply decreased. Nothing in sight suggests any increase in inflation. Why should workers assume 5% inflation and demand higher wages, setting in motion the inflationary spiral?

Milton Friedman was a mad scientist. His goal was to discredit any policy of active management of the business cycle. He set in motion the wage and price increases that cycle up the spiral of inflation. He knew perfectly well what would be the result, and he actually predicted it, but blamed the inflation on the imaginary demons of active monetary policy.

KEYNESIAN ECONOMICS: THE MISSING STEP

Irving Fisher explained very well how the mechanism of the business cycle works in his book *Booms and Depressions*, which he published in 1932, four years before Keynes published his General Theory. Fisher made an excellent diagnosis of the economic disease of depression, but could not offer a sure-fire cure. Still, he made the great contribution to the understanding of the business cycle by explaining that accumulation of debt to commercial banks leads to economic prosperity, and liquidation of debt leads to an economic depression. Fisher also explained that a fall in wages and prices cannot increase demand because deflation makes debt bigger in real terms (a farmer, for example, has to sell two bushels of wheat instead of one to pay the same amount of debt in dollars), which leads to lower prices, still more selling, still lower prices and so on in circles (the debt-deflation spiral). Keynes, for some unknown reason, chose to ignore Irving Fisher's theory as a whole, but he did pick up a few small segments of it—consumers, for some reason, decide to keep more cash trying to save money, which leads to lower spending and lower demand—without even mentioning Irving Fisher's name. By the way, FDR's administration started the New Deal programs under the influence of Irving Fisher, and not Keynes, who arrived at the party much later, when his General Theory was published in 1936, halfway through the Depression. At any rate, Keynes also made a great contribution to economic theory with his narrow-minded focus on the aggregate demand. After reading *Booms and Depressions* by Irving Fisher, only a lunatic will say that mutual raiding by banks and their customers is a healthy market action leading to a better economy, and Keynes was not a lunatic. He did recognize that government action was needed, but his proposed solution was weak.

Irving Fisher explained that by the time of his writing not only was the money supply falling, but the velocity of money was falling too, so the cumulative effect was that the economy was functioning at about one third of its pre-depression level. The economy was dead in the water, and very strong action was required. Keynes proposed the government borrow money on the market in order to finance Public Works—that solution was used by British during the Potato Famine in Ireland, and even though it did save many lives, it was not nearly enough. The weakness of this solution is the weak point of Keynesian economics. Only a very massive injection of money into the economy could do the job, but how can you inject the money if that money is supposed to be backed by gold which you don't have?

The missing step in the Keynesian theory is the recognition of the fact that a monetary system based on the gold standard is not only inherently unstable, but is also very difficult to improve when liquidation of debt picks up speed in a debt-deflation spiral.

This recognition is implicit in Fisher's writing. He came close to suggesting the abolishment of the gold standard when, at the end of his book, he proposed creating a monetary system based on a stable dollar which would be backed not by gold, but by an index of commodities. To me, that looks like a polite way of suggesting the abandonment of the gold standard and using money that represents claims on the whole wealth of the country, which we have today.

Keynes, on the other hand, ignored this problem entirely. One would hope the new Keynesian theory would revisit this issue and set the record straight. It would be easy to argue that Keynes was fundamentally right about injecting money into the economy, but a monetary system based on the gold standard would render this nearly impossible. Unfortunately, the new Keynesian theory drags us into an irrational discussion about the rationality of economic decisions, and is even suggesting that if only people could open their eyes, consider the facts, and lower their prices and wages. When people decide to hold more cash, then the slump in output and employment becomes self-correcting.

But Fisher explained that lower prices and wages means deflation, which makes debt larger and more difficult to pay back, which in turn leads to bankruptcies and forces the liquidation of assets, which leads to still lower prices, still bigger debt, still more depressed sales, and so on. Why should new Keynesians accept the monetarist doctrine that lower prices and wages will increase the real value of money, and people will not need more money, and in the long run it would cure the economy instead of burning it in the furnace of the debt-deflation spiral? Why use the recycled goods of monetarism which was made out of the recycled trash of the classical theory that an economy based on the free market is always self-correcting, and will cure itself in the long run?

Of course, it will cure itself in the long run when banks have already bankrupted half of the population, and have already bought as many real assets as they could at very reduced prices. That is why the Glass-Steagall Act 1933 prohibited commercial banks from owning insurance companies and investment banks, because commercial banks had incentives to cut lending to the economy, to choke it into an economic depression, and then to make loans to the investment companies they owned to buy anything and everything valuable insight, pennies on the dollar.

Let's open our eyes. Suppose, you recently bought a house with a mortgage loan; you have also car payments; and you bought home appliances and furniture with a credit card, on which you make only minimum payments. Now, the economy hit a bump. Following the advice of new Keynesians and monetarists, everyone is dropping their wages and prices to cure the economy. Your wages dropped by 10%, but the purchasing power is the same as before, so you don't need more money. But the nominal amount of your payments remains the same; there is no discount for the deflation. Now, what will you liquidate first?

THE CASE FOR ESTABLISHING A CENTRAL BANK OF THE UNITED STATES

Our Federal Reserve System, which functions as the Central Bank of the U.S. is actually a private institution, even though it is under significant control of our federal government. Any other central bank in the world is owned by the national government of that country. The United States of America also needs to have a central bank owned by the federal government. The obvious solution is to nationalize the Federal Reserve System. The reasons are many. One is to stop the rumors that the Fed is still owned by Great Britain, or some bankers from there, by the Illuminati, or by some Jews in Israel, etc. The American public has dozens of amazing and amusing tales about the Fed.

The second reason is that the central bank will be able to finance large projects which our biggest banks will not want to go anywhere near. Take, for example, Central California. It does not have enough water to grow fruits, nuts, and vegetables. Northern California has so much water flowing down from the Sierra mountains, and most of it flows into the Pacific Ocean. We need low interest financing for a project to build a waterway to redirect the water from Northern to Central California. It will cost a few billion dollars. The loan would be paid by California in the next ten or fifteen years. Money will be collected from the farmers as fees for water and in taxes.

Now, here is the question. Why should the central bank of the U.S. provide a low interest loan to farmers in central California? Why not hire some investment bankers in New York who will raise money for you in the bond market? There are a couple of good reasons. Investment bankers are not cheap to hire, and the interest rate will not be low. If the farmers save a billion dollars on investment bankers fees and on the interest over the life of the loan, it would be a good chunk of savings for them. We know that all costs are one way or another always passed on to the consumers. If we make it unnecessarily expensive for farmers, we will pay higher prices for the fruit, nuts, and veggies they grow. It's that simple.

Another question. Why should we increase inflation by printing money for the farmers? First of all, the growing economy needs more money supply. Second, only a gift of printed currency would permanently increase the money supply. A loan will increase the money supply temporarily, and it will be reduced when the loan is paid back. In the end, we will pay lower prices on the whole for our fruits, nuts, and veggies. Prices may be higher in nominal terms, but they will be lower than if we do not help them with low interest financing.

Reasonable people, especially investment bankers, will argue that the government should not decide to provide subsidies to some group of people and not to another. We should disagree. We have been providing subsidies to farmers for a very long time. This low interest loan would be just another type of subsidy, and millions of Americans will hopefully become healthier consuming more fruits and vegetables. I'd venture to guess that in the long term the health benefits will be worth many times more than we give to the farmers as a loan subsidy. This is an example of a project that we should subsidize with low interest loans in the name of the public interest.

Another example of a project that deserves a low interest rate subsidy from the central bank is to build modern new cities with public transportation where most people will not even need to own a car, and here is the reasoning: we are building around one million single family homes every year, and we are covering the surface of the Earth with those houses and with highways, roads, and streets leading to them. Because of this relentless expansion of the suburbs we are losing agricultural land and open space. At some point in the future we will not have enough agricultural land to feed the growing population. The result will be poverty just like in those overpopulated countries where people work the whole day for a couple of bowls of rice. We need to save the agricultural land and open space, and limit immigration. We cannot separate these economic issues because they affect each other. Do we want to cut down all our forests to make room for more suburbs? Plus, suburban housing is neither cost effective, nor does it make us much happier. The lines of infrastructure—electricity, water, sewer, etc., —are too long, too expensive to build, and contribute to higher costs. We sit in traffic for hours, and every year more people are killed in auto accidents than we lost in the entire Vietnam War. Many thousands more are not killed, but are crippled and paralyzed. Is this the best type of living we can imagine?

We can build modern new cities where residential city blocks are one square mile. High-rise apartment buildings are located at the perimeter of the block. In the middle of the block there are most of what we need on a day to day basis—schools, medical centers, shopping centers, after school facilities, gyms, etc. Children will walk to school, and not ride in SUVs on slippery winter roads. The perimeter of one square mile is four miles long; it is a lot of room to build high-rise apartment buildings. On the street level of those buildings there will be all kinds of services, from barbershops to restaurants, etc. There will also be industrial blocks, commercial blocks, green zones, and whatever the city planners suggest. All city blocks will be about the same size, like on a chess board. Speedy trolleys will move people along the straight lines, and the trolley lines will be on all four sides of every city block. We can imagine that trolleys will not need human conductors; they can be automated. A city that is ten blocks long and ten blocks wide will have one hundred blocks. With only one half of them residential, the city will have about two million residents, and the footprint of only one hundred square miles, which is much, much smaller than a typical suburb of that capacity, with the same population. This type of city planning will allow many people to work on the same block in which they live. Those who have to travel to other blocks, including industrial and commercial areas, will take the trolleys which will be designed to have enough room, and will run frequently. People will save tons of money on transportation, and there will be many other benefits. We are burning an absolutely incredible amount of gasoline in our cars, which pollutes the air in our cities. Los Angeles is a giant gas chamber. Sprawling, disorganized city planning is not only expensive, but very harmful for our health. Also, the whole world is concerned about global warming. If America demonstrates that this type of city planning makes car ownership not necessary for most people, many countries around the world will follow American leadership. At the time when American leadership is increasingly questioned by even our NATO allies in Europe, this bold new initiative to build modern, practical, and economical new cities is very much desirable. America will be able to claim credit for environmental leadership, and most countries in the world will be able to build cities of this type as it will not require much high-technology.

An interesting question is whether the construction of modern cities can be used as public works if and when the next economic depression arrives. It will be very problematic for the following reasons: we will have to increase capacity of the construction materials industry and keep it idle and available for future use. The same is true of the construction labor force. We will have to train millions of future construction workers, and then keep them in other jobs. But suppose that we manage to keep one million construction workers in reserves, and available when necessary. How much can we achieve? If an average construction worker earns $30,000 per year, then one million workers will earn one million times that amount, which is ($30,000 times 1,000,000) $30 billion. It is only a 30 billion dollar increase to our GDP. During the Great Depression the money supply was falling for the first couple of years by more than 10% per year. If our money supply drops by 10%, then an increase by making $30 billion in the construction industry would be just a big pipe dream. It is scary even to think about our money supply dropping by 10%. $30 billion will amount to a foot massage to an economy that is having a heart attack. Public works were not an adequate response to the Potato Famine in Ireland, and it will not be any more effective in today's economy.

We have only one choice: to not allow a debt-deflation spiral to develop. If the liquidation of debt starts for some reason, the only reasonable solution is to make emergency loans to all big and middle-sized banks. We should not call it a bailout, because loans will be returned as soon as the panic goes away. Making even a $100 billion loan to a bank is quick and easy. Just promise to return the loan, and here is the increase of your account in the Fed. It will take literally a few keystrokes on the Fed's computer system. The whole banking system would need a few trillion dollars in emergency loans. Why so much? Let's take a look at the pyramid. Money supply—the total amount of money in circulation—is maybe ten times the amount of bank reserves. That money supply circulates a number of times every year, and that number is the velocity of money. It is very easy to create an economic recession. The economy might be very healthy, with 100% employment, but say the GDP drops a small amount. This small drop will generate negative comments by talking heads, some of whom might have political agendas. The economy will start contracting. We already know how the economy can go in circles down the toilet. That is why we should stop calculating and reporting our GDP. It is a tool of destruction.

Another concern is commercial banks gambling with depositor's money. There are all kinds of exotic contracts, the result of financial engineering. They all should be prohibited, because even a modest loss by one bank might create a panicked response and start a run on the banks. And that is when the Fed will need to make emergency loans, because there are $10 in deposits against $1 in reserves, and any attempt to withdraw even $1 out of $10 in deposits will start mutual raiding, when banks raid their customers before the customers raid the banks. Now, the problem with the Fed making emergency loans is that some of the banks had probably made losing bets, and they are bankrupt. To determine which banks are good and which banks are gamblers and losers will take days, if not weeks. If there is a financial panic, everyone will want an emergency loan, but why should the Fed loan billions of dollars to gamblers who will just pay their gambling debt and go bankrupt anyway? This is why exotic contracts should be prohibited. Banks should just make loans to the economy. Then the Fed will be more likely to assume that the emergency loans will not go to cover gambling debts.

How can we force the banks to stop gambling? The problem here is that banks are no longer just banks. The Banking Act of 1933, also known as the Glass-Steagall Act, prohibited commercial banks from owning insurance companies and investment banks. In 1999, President Clinton, the Fed chairman Greenspan, and Congress enacted a law that, in effect, killed the Glass-Steagall Act. Now commercial banks are again allowed to own other financial institutions which are free to invest on their own accounts, and there is no longer a wall of separation between them. The banks can make loans to their insurance companies and investment banks who do the investing. As we see, there are many opportunities for things to go wrong, for a panic to develop, and for an urgent need for emergency loans to arise, even if no one conspires to sell "goats" to each other, collecting bonuses for paper profits and leaving the shareholders to hold the bag. But what if the Fed refuses to provide emergency loans at the time of financial panic, like when Lehman Brothers went bankrupt in the fall of 2008? Actually, the Fed was not very quick, and it allowed the panic to increase for a full year. The worst time was in the fall of 2008. The problem here is the big banks have a lot of influence over the Fed, because it is still a private institution. If and when a depression starts, some big banks might want to prolong it and to buy assets pennies on the dollar, and the Fed will be able to find all kinds of excuses not to help the economy. That is why we need to do three things. First, prohibit gambling by commercial banks. Second, enact another

Glass-Steagall Act in order to separate banks from other financial institutions. Third, nationalize the Fed.

The next concern is interest rates. For almost four decades, from around 1980 to the present time, interest rates have been falling. Falling interest rates are always positive for the economy for a number of reasons. First, low interest rates mean affordable financing. As the Fed raises the short-term interest rates, it affects all interest rates, including 10-year notes and 30-year bonds. As the interest rates of Treasuries rise, depositors are inclined to take their money out of the bank and buy Treasuries, reducing the bank reserves. The banks then are under pressure to increase the interest rates on deposits. We should note that when depositors buy Treasuries from their bank, then the money—and the bank reserves—stay in the same bank. Even if depositors buy Treasuries in a different place, the total reserves of the banking system stay the same as reserves simply move from one bank to another. Only if the Treasuries are bought from the Fed are the total reserves of commercial banks reduced. Those banks that do not have Treasuries on their balance sheet will be under pressure to increase interest rates to their depositors, and they themselves will have an excuse to increase interest rates on loans. As interest rates rise, financing becomes less affordable. The risk of investment increases, and business investment falls. The economy will be facing a headwind in an uphill battle.

The second reason is that the cost/benefit ratio becomes risky. Investment, employment, and output will all be slowing down. We already know about GDP, which should not even be calculated and reported. If interest rates continue to rise—two steps up, one step down—for another ten years, the economy will be in bad shape.

Use any mortgage calculator on the internet. Enter a $100,000 mortgage loan at 5% and see your monthly payments and the price of a home you can afford. Next, change the interest rate on your mortgage loan to 10%, and see what difference it makes. The price of a home you can afford drops, even though the monthly payment stays the same. The same effect can be applied to all assets in the economy. Higher interest rates mean low prices, less construction, lower output, and higher unemployment. Higher interest rates push prices down, but lower output means lower aggregate supply, which pushes prices up. Most likely, we will have both higher unemployment and higher prices. Don't blame the President, unless the Fed has already been nationalized. The President can ask the Central Bank politely to please increase their purchases of Treasuries, which increases reserves of the commercial banks.

The point here is that at the present time big banks own the financial companies which can be used to buy assets in a deeply depressed economy. Big banks once again have incentives to choke the economy into an economic depression and to keep making loans to the financial companies they own rather than to businesses in the economy. In the case of the economy being knocked down into a depression with a vicious debt-deflation spiral, emergency loans will have to be made in a very short period of time. For all these reasons, the United States needs to establish a central bank owned and operated by the federal government.

THE GREAT DEPRESSION OF 2020: HOW TO AVOID IT

There are quite a few reasons why the Second Great Depression is very likely. Let's begin with two basic assertions. First, we should recognize that not everyone suffers during economic downturns. For some financial institutions a severe economic downturn would present a wonderful opportunity to buy all kinds of assets —stocks, bonds, real estate—pennies on the dollar. Let's call it evil intent. Second, we should recognize that some financial institutions do have the means to knock the economy down into an economic depression and to benefit from it, but the potential for evil intent is not a consideration in any of the major economic theories.

Now let's take a look at the reasons why the Second Great Depression is very likely in the not too distant future:

1. After the Second World War economic downturns have taken place every 10 years, plus or minus a year or two. An economic downturn is not the same thing as an economic recession, which means a decline in production and employment for two consecutive quarters. An economic downturn might not include a recession, but when the economy moves one step forward in one quarter, but two steps back in the next quarter, and cannot move forward steadily for a few quarters, that is an economic downturn. Economic downturns have taken place around 1950, 1960, 1970, 1980, 1990, 2000, 2010, and the next downturn is "scheduled" for 'round 2020.

2. After the financial crisis that started in 2007, big commercial banks bought quite a few brokerage firms. Now big commercial banks have an incentive to cause an economic depression, as their brokerage houses can act as investment departments of their parent companies and will be able to buy assets pennies on the dollar. The Banking Act of 1933 required the separation of investment banking and commercial banking functions. The Glass-Steagall Act, as The Banking Act is known, was enacted during the worst year of the Great Depression because it was widely recognized that commercial banks would rather make loans to their investment departments to buy assets at low prices, but not loans to the real economy. In 1999, Wall Street managed to convince President Clinton and the Congress that the separation of investment banking and commercial banking

functions was no longer needed. In 2007, big banks bought brokerage houses. The ducks are being put in a row. The question is, do these sitting ducks suspect anything?

1. International bankers have reached agreements known as Basel I, Basel II, and Basel III. The latest one, Basel III, requires all systemically vital (too big to fail) commercial banks to increase capital significantly by the year 2020. The word "capital" has different meanings even in a context such as monetary system and banking. It can mean the difference between assets and liabilities, which is called either equity or net worth, or simply capital (company's own capital). But Basel bankers mean something entirely different. They mean bank reserves against which banks make loans. Any significant increase in the percentage of reserves, required to be kept in order to satisfy withdrawal demands, will cause a magnified decrease in bank lending, lower money supply, lower aggregate demand, then the vicious debt-deflation spiral, and, ultimately, a worldwide economic depression. Consider the following: If banks are required to keep 10% of deposits in reserve, they can lend $100 in loans, keeping $10 in reserves. If the required reserves are increased from 10% up to, say, 15%, then the banks will be required to keep $15 in reserves against $100 in deposits.

2. But how does one increase reserves? There are two ways. The first way is to increase interest rates offered to depositors, and add the cash to the reserves. This will not work because most of the cash is already in the banking system, and has already been deposited. The second way is to start collecting debt without making new loans. That is exactly what will deliver a fatal blow to the world economy. Liquidation of debt. Debt-

deflation spiral. This is what caused the first Great Depression. This is what will cause the second one. Read "*Booms and Depressions*" by Irving Fisher. He was the greatest economist of the last, or any, century. Irving Fisher's theory is the foundation of both monetarism and Keynesianism. Fisher explained very clearly that liquidation of debt causes lower money supply and lower aggregate demand. To argue that either lower money supply (monetarism) or lower aggregate demand (Keynesianism) caused the Great Depression is clear evidence of intellectual dishonesty of both schools of economics thought. A good question is whether Basel international bankers are educated well enough to know Irving Fisher's Theory. Do they really not know it? Or is there evil intent?

3. How to avoid the second Great Depression. Let's start with what will not work if the economic downturn has already started. Monetarist theory will not work. Friedman's assertion that the Federal Reserve failed to inject cash into the economy is flawed because at that time the monetary system was based on the gold standard. The Fed did not have a legal right just to print paper money and to make loans to commercial banks. Now, in the 21st century, the situation is much improved. Our monetary system is no longer based on the gold standard. The Fed has a right to print currency and to buy Treasury securities. The Fed gets more Treasuries, and the commercial banks increase their reserves, against which the banks can make loans.

4. Will it work? No. If the bankers do, indeed, have evil intent to cause economic depression, they will be selling their Treasuries to the Fed, they will be increasing their bank reserves, but they will be sitting on their reserves, collecting debt and not making new loans. The

explanation for public consumption? The economy is not good, and making new loans is risky. When the economy is deep in the depression, the big banks will make loans to the brokerage firms they own to buy assets at low prices. If, on the other hand, we assume that the top management of big banks and Basel bankers are simply dumb, and they are paid millions of dollars for knowing nothing in particular about the banking business and the economy, then the economic depression will take place, not as a result of evil intent, but as a result of innocent incompetence. Monetarism, for example, does not take into account artificial demand created when banks pre-qualify millions of would-be home buyers to buy a limited quantity of homes available on a market, whipping up artificial demand without increasing money supply.

There are a few things that we can do to avoid the second Great Depression. First, we need to eliminate the incentives for bankers to cause an economic depression. We need to separate the investment banking and the commercial banking functions. It will take time. If the economic downturn starts before that, the commercial banks should not be allowed to make loans to their brokerage firms, or invest in assets by any other means. Economic depressions are characterized by lower money supply, lower demand, and high unemployment. If the economic downturn becomes severe, we can nationalize the Federal Reserve System and create a Central Bank of the United States, which will be owned and controlled by our federal government.

But there still will be the same problem. The Central Bank will be able to print currency and to buy Treasuries, or simply make loans to a few selected banks, but no one can force the banks to make loans if they have evil intent. Then we can create a

Commercial Bank owned by the federal government. It will not deal with the public deposits like regular commercial banks. It will take billion-dollar loans straight from the Central Bank and make billion dollars loans to real estate developers to build modern new cities. Housing is too expensive. We need to increase the supply of housing. Also, a Central Bank can finance infrastructure projects like high-speed railroads, at very low interest rates. To build a web of high-speed railroad lines across America would cost, probably, a few trillion dollars over a few decades it will take to build it. The commercial banks have neither capital nor any desire to finance such huge infrastructure projects.

WHAT IS WRONG WITH EUROPE

What exactly is wrong with the European Union? Let's skip banal platitudes and generalities and get straight to the point.

First, let's take a quick look at the current situation. Prices on government debt are rising, and yields are falling for long-term debt. At the present time, in July of 2019, the yield on 10-year German debt is negative at minus 0.3% (-0.3%). It means that if you buy that bond, you will get back less money than you paid for the bond. A 10-year Switzerland bond has the lowest yield at minus 0.5% (-0.5%). You have to pay them 5 Euros per year for the privilege to lend them money with a one-thousand Euros bond. It is clear that the financial world is upside down, but what is going on?

In theory, the price of a bond should reflect expected inflation, real interest rate desired (nominal interest rate minus expected inflation), and the risk of default. Suppose, risk of default of German debt is zero, so there is no risk premium. Nominal interest rate on ten-year bonds is (-0.3%). Let's assume very low expected inflation at only 1% per year. To break even, we need both profit and loss to equal zero. We are losing purchasing power with both negative interest rates and inflation. The total loss equals 0.3%+1%=1.3%, but this is expected loss, not real loss because we don't know the future.

Let's ask the following question. Who buys those bonds to lose money? The European Central Bank prints euros and buys government bonds of all countries of the Eurozone, but the ECB has a legal limit of 33% for government debt of any one country. According to *The Economist* (July 13th, 2019, briefing), in the case of Germany it is already at 29%. It means that the ECB already owns 29% of Germany's government bonds. There is not much room to continue buying government debt, pushing prices up and interest down. Even Greece's 10-yr government bonds pay only 2.3%. If inflation in Greece hits 2%, then those who invested in that country's government bonds will make no profit.

So, what does it all mean? It can only mean one thing. Big boys of the financial industry do not expect inflation. They know that there will be deflation. With deflation will come the debt-deflation spiral which we have already discussed in this book in great details. Liquidation of debt.

Now, what can be done? In the United States, we can put our central bank under full control of the federal government. We can force the central bank to gradually increase construction loans to build modern new cities. If we start in 2020, then in a few years we can gradually increase the amount of construction loans to hundreds of billions of dollars. If liquidation of debt takes place regardless, we can force the central bank to make zero- interest loans to all S&P 500 companies. The companies will be happy to retire their debt and to make new investments, but this liquidation of debt will not cause decrease of money supply, lower aggregate demand, and economic depression.

The European Union can be described as the United States of Europe. They have their own currency, the euro, their own Central Bank. They also have very interesting economic problems.

Economic problems of Europe stem from the fact that they don't have the financial system in place. Imagine for one minute that the U.S. does not have a Treasury Department that sells Treasury securities, which represent debt of the federal government. Instead, the Fed is buying the debt of all states, separately. That is what the EU is doing, economic integration without financial integration. Such a system is inherently very unstable.

Imagine for a minute that liquidation of debt started in the EU. The economy is collapsing. What the EU is likely to do? Will they force the ECB to print money and make construction loans to build modern new cities in Italy where standard of living has not increased for decades? Will they force the ECB to print money and make interest-free loans to hundreds of biggest companies? If not, then the whole of the EU will go down the toilet, with the ECB absolutely independent.

The biggest puzzle in economics is why creators of dumb economic theories—Keynes, Milton Friedman, Robert Lucas, etc. —received recognition and Noble prices, but the greatest economist of the 20th century did not. His theory of the debt-deflation spiral has been suppressed, part of it shamelessly stolen by Keynes (aggregate demand), and Milton Friedman (money supply). These two economists have created two competing schools of economic thought. Keynesians argue that the aggregate demand is the most important part of the economy. Monetarists argue that the money supply is most important. We have already discussed in this book that money supply and aggregate demand are simply the two sides of the same coin. It is very clear in Irving

Fisher's debt-deflation spiral theory. But the dismal science is still in the Dark Ages.

Even *The Economist*, arguably the most competent publication about economics, is fishing in muddy water. The following quote is from the Briefing about the world economy, July 13th, 2019. "Modern economics says business cycles are caused by changes in total spending which outpace the ability of prices and wages to respond. Recessions happen when, faced with lower spending, firms sell less and shed workers, leading spending to fall yet further, rather than adjust prices and wages so as to balance supply and demand." This quote is very misleading and logically incoherent. In *Booms and Depressions*, which was published almost 90 years ago, Irving Fisher explained that if a businessman's profits "are squeezed too thin for comfort, naturally he will cut his production and release some of his employees.... employment will take a slump." This is the sixth main factor. But "rather than adjust prices and wages so as to balance supply and demand" suggests that during the economic downturn both prices and wages should be adjusted downward. This was the main argument of classical economists both before and during the Great Depression, until Irving Fisher explained that lower prices and wages make debt more difficult to pay off, and lead to liquidation of debt and economic depression that feeds on itself.

If even *The Economist* tells us this nonsense, it means that the world economy is, indeed, in grave danger. Economists should forget discredited classical economics and start discussing how to keep prices and wages reasonably stable. Reading *Booms and Depressions* should be the very first step for any policymaker whose decisions might affect the economy. It must be required reading for anyone who studies economics.

There are interesting problems in the EU. Why, for example, Italy is so miserable in the EU? Given the fact that many countries of the Eastern Europe joined the EU, it can be explained by the fact that their standard of living must go up before Italy's. At the present time, and for two decades that the EU exists, most of the investment was going to poorer countries of the EU, where wages were much lower. Large outflows of the financial capital from Italy to the Eastern Europe can be one reason. A second, but related, reason is that Germany has a large export industry and the current account balance is at 8% of the GDP. Outflows of the financial capital are most likely much smaller than inflows. Italy has a much smaller export industry and the current account balance is only positive 2% of GDP. Outflows of the financial capital are very likely much larger than inflows. If Italian investors invest a lot of capital in other countries, it means that Italian commercial banks have lower reserves to make loans. Without the sufficient amount of loans, the economy is weak. There should be no great mystery in determining the main reasons of Italian economy's weakness.

If, on the other hand, the main reason is too much of bad loans as a result of both corruption and organized crime, then economists cannot do anything. If this is, indeed, the case, then Italy should be allowed to leave the EU and rot on its own.

And the last point. Germany has a large influence on the monetary policy of the ECB. For Germans, to print currency means to increase inflation, but that is a mistake. Germany has a current - account surplus at 8% of GDP. Like a giant vacuum cleaner, Germany is sucking in monetary savings of other countries of the EU, leaving them financially weaker with smaller amounts of bank reserves.

There is only one solution. The ECB should print currency, euros, and make construction loans to build whatever the EU needs. There will be no increase in inflation in the long run because loans will be paid back. The only alternative is to disband the EU if and when a severe economic downturn comes along. It would be a shame to destroy the EU after surviving two decades of existence.

NEGATIVE INTEREST RATES IN EUROPE

It is October, 2019. Interest rates on 10-year Treasury bonds are at 1.5%. Unemployment is at 3.5% in the U.S. For the Euro area average unemployment rate was 7.4% in August, but in Germany only 3.1%. The average interest rates for 10-year government bonds in the Euro area is minus 0.6%. It means that investors are losing 0.6% of their money every year. These statistics might seem boring, but it is extremely important to understand what is going on, especially because the commentators are not providing correct explanations either because they really don't understand the situation, or they are misleading the public on purpose.

You might read in the media that the root cause of low interest rates in the Euro area is an excess of saving over spending, and Germans' obsession with frugality bears much of the blame. This is total nonsense and brainwashing. Income minus spending equals saving.

First, about monetary saving and spending. There is a certain amount of currency in circulation. People deposit their savings in a bank, and that amount of currency is destroyed, but an equal amount is added to bank reserves against which the bank makes loans which increase the money supply by the same amount. The borrowed money circulates in the economy. Consumers buy something, and their monetary savings decrease, but savings of manufacturers and retailers increase by the same amount. Businesses pay wages to their workers, and the monetary savings move in the opposite direction. Your spending becomes my savings, and vice versa. Every business transaction involves equal amounts of spending and savings. In the economy as a whole the total amount of monetary savings does not change. Total spending, on the other hand, is increasing with each transaction when the same monetary units are moving in the economy to pay for different transactions.

What happens if the workers spend only, say, 90% of their wages? Here we have higher income and lower spending, which means excess of income over spending, and that excess will be deposited to a bank and will increase bank reserves, against which the bank can now make loans.

To whom? Consumers don't need loans; they have savings in the bank. Businesses are in a situation where they pay workers 100 euros in wages but get only 90 euros in income. This means that over time the businesses will run out of money. They don't need loans to invest in slow business. The economy hits a brick wall. The writing on the wall says "imbalance." Or "disequilibrium," if you prefer. The only way forward is to drive around the brick wall. But first, about interest rates.

Interest rates are determined by several factors. The most important are the expected inflation and risk of default. This is true for ordinary loans, but in the financing of government spending the interest rates are determined more by the central bank. When the central bank buys government securities, their prices go up, and the same securities pay lower interest. Bankers have a lovely expression for this process, "quantitative easing," probably because QE increases the quantity of banking reserves when banks' government securities are exchanged for the central bank's money. So, QE increases reserves of commercial banks, but is also pushing prices of government securities up and interest rates down. Interest rates on government debt influence interest rates banks pay to their depositors.

The European Central Bank prints Euros and buys government debt of a few big-spender countries, pushing prices up and interest rates down. The result is that 10-year government bonds in Greece, which is basically bankrupt, pay about the same interest as U.S. 10-year Treasury Bonds. This situation cannot last much longer. A couple of big-spender countries like Greece and Italy will leave the EU. The ECB will not be allowed to print euros and buy junk debt at inflated prices forever.

But what is the alternative? Now the ECB prints Euros and buys bonds of individual countries with the goal to give the governments more money to spend, and to stimulate their economies. This is a classic Keynesian solution to the problem of a slowing economy—to increase government spending. And here the discussion becomes very interesting—and more complicated.

Keynes developed his theory as a solution to the economic depression. His solution was for the government to borrow money and to spend it as a means of increasing aggregate demand. At that time America was on the gold standard, and Keynes could not suggest printing currency. His suggestion to borrow was the best solution among very bad options. Also, the solution was for economic depression, and not for the slowing economy when the unemployment rate is very low by historical standards.

Still, there are very important parallels. Economic depressions, after all, are just very bad versions of a slowing economy. The same fundamental forces are at work—low consumer spending, low business spending, etc.—we'll call it a brick wall. Now, how should a slowing economy go around a brick wall.

The ECB prints Euros to buy bonds. Money is injected into the economy, which was the primary goal, but the side effect is that bond prices went through the roof, and bond yields—the interest paid—fell through the floor. The problem here is that this version of Keynesianism is outdated and inefficient. In Germany, bonds yields are already negative, and we are not in a depression yet.

This way around the wall leads to a dead end. If commercial banks reduce interest, they pay on deposits to zero, depositors will withdraw their deposits, and banks will be left with only their own capital. This road leads to an economic depression, but there is a better way around the brick wall

Our goal is to eliminate negative factors that are present in misused Keynesian theory while trying to achieve the same objective: stimulation of the economy through increase in aggregate demand. The negative factors are:

1. When a central bank buys government bonds with printed currency, the currency goes to increase the reserves of commercial banks, which may or may not increase lending in the economy that is approaching the brick wall.

2. When commercial banks sell their inventory of government bonds, the government will issue more bonds and get deeper into the swamp of debt. In this case the government will spend money, but not necessarily to build anything useful, and do so at the cost of increasing government debt which at some point might become unmanageable.

3. Low or negative bond yields may provoke commercial banks to reduce interest rates on deposits to zero. If depositors withdraw enough deposits, an economic depression will be guaranteed.

Europe needs an emergency law to prohibit commercial banks from paying interest on deposits lower than 1%. If one or two small banks die, it is a small price to pay for eliminating the danger of depression. After that, Europe should create one commercial bank owned by not any of the countries, but rather by the government of the European Union. The commercial bank will borrow reserves straight from the ECB and make loans at low interest rates to build useful projects. It might be hotels and restaurants in Greece, so that Europeans will have long and affordable vacations. To finance private industry of vacations in Greece is better than to finance its government, even if loans will be made at zero percent. The whole of Europe will benefit from such loans.

Europe, and the whole world, need to discard the puritanical version of Keynesianism and adopt its modified version. It will allow the economies to rid themselves of all three negative factors in the puritanical version, but will retain the same goal of stimulating the economy, it will be achieved by direct financing of private industry instead of wasteful spending by governments. Most of the loans will be productive, will be increasing standard of living, and will create millions of jobs. This is the right way to go around the brick wall.

During the last economic downturn which started in 2008 and lasted a couple of years, it became clear that something was not right with the world economy. I would argue that the worst part of the world economy are the commonly accepted economic theories. The worst misconception is that poor countries need to borrow billions and billions of dollars or euros from rich countries in order to improve their economies.

It never works. Poor countries borrow dollars and start to invest in their economies. First, they have to exchange the borrowed dollars for the local currency because local workers get their wages in local currency, and not in dollars. As a result, the exchange rate of the local currency goes up, its purchasing power improves, imported goods become less expensive, and inflation goes down. When the government is done exchanging dollars, everything goes in reverse. The exchange rate of the local currency drops, inflation increases, and no one understands that borrowing dollars and exchanging them for local currency is very much like getting drunk. The economy gets intoxicated, everyone feels high, but sooner or later they're in hangover.

The right way to borrow would be to borrow only a limited amount in dollars to buy investment goods. For a simplified example, consider the following. Suppose, a country in Africa is dirt poor, but it has more than enough dirt—or agricultural land—to grow hemp. Hemp is a plant that grows almost everywhere without pesticides. It can be used to manufacture clothing like jeans and jackets, ladies' handbags, the tops of shoes, and many other things. The country might start growing hemp, but it needs a factory in order to manufacture textiles made with hemp. The country is well advised to proceed in one of the two ways. Either allow a foreign company to build and operate the new factory, or borrow dollars to buy the machinery for the factory. In this case borrowing is for investment, and not consumption

Compare this approach with what Argentina did a few times already. Argentina borrows money, but most of the borrowed money is spent on consumption, and not investment. Every time there was a default, and lenders suffered huge losses, which is the only positive thing coming out of this reckless borrowing, because dumb lenders do deserve to suffer losses.

Suppose now, our small African nation is growing hemp very successfully, but the country needs to build small towns in faraway areas where the hemp is grown so that workers and their families can live close to their place of work. The question here is how to finance the construction of housing. If the country doesn't need to import any construction machinery or materials, should this country borrow dollars to finance the construction of housing? The answer is no. The central bank should print local currency and make a loan to a commercial bank, which, in return, will make a loan to a reliable construction company or a real estate developer to build the necessary housing. As money starts spreading through the country's economy, the aggregate demand will increase and stimulate the whole economy. Some of the new money will be added to savings accounts of individuals, increasing the bank reserves against which commercial banks will be able to make mortgage loans. As long as there is an unemployed labor force, the central bank will be able to print local currency and create productive jobs to increase the living standards of the population. If a poor country wants its population to have decent housing and "a chicken in every pot," that country doesn't need to borrow foreign currency to build housing and chicken farms. Its own central bank should finance the economic expansion without accumulating debilitating foreign debt.

Now, what does this example of a poor African country have to do with economic problems in Europe? Well, there is a common theme. The European Central Bank (ECB) should start printing euros and making loans to finance whatever Europe needs, be that a defense factory in France or chicken farms in Eastern Europe. Of course, the financing should go through commercial banks. This means that a few commercial banks should be able to borrow their reserves straight from the ECB. As long as there is an unemployed labor force, the ECB should make loans to create productive jobs. Countries like Greece and Italy will be better served by such loans. At the present time the ECB prints euros and buys government bonds from European countries like Greece and Italy, which are deeply in debt. This is a flawed economic policy. The main instrument of economic policy should be loans to create productive jobs. Buying government bonds of prolific spenders only encourages them to continue spending. Still, Europe needs to create government bonds that represent an obligation of the whole Euro zone, so that the ECB will be able to finance its spending.

IMPLICATIONS OF MODIFIED KEYNESIANISM

Modified Keynesian theory offers tremendous advantages to any country (or currency union like European Union). At the root, the idea is very simple. Central banks print currencies and buy government debt from commercial banks. The commercial banks are used as a fig leaf to conceal the simple truth that the Fed, for example, buys of from the federal government and pays with currency received from the federal government (The Treasury Department) for the cost of printing currency, for all practical purposes, is free because the Fed can order the printing and delivery of an unlimited amount of currency which can then be used to pay for anything. When the Fed buys Treasuries, reserves of commercial banks increase, which increase the total amount of loans—if the banks decide to make more loans against increased reserves.

In this convoluted financial system, currency is printed to buy government debt. Any attempt to reduce government debt will necessarily involve a drastic reduction in government borrowing which will cause lower money supply and economic depression. All those politicians who agitate for the reduction of federal debt do not have a clue what they're talking about. We are using a system of perpetual stimulation of the economy which perpetually increases federal debt.

A modified Keynesian economic policy allows for the arresting of federal debt at the present level. Borrowing by the federal government will be replaced by private-sector borrowing. If we replace a $1 trillion federal budget deficit with $1 trillion in borrowing by the private sector, the federal budget deficit will equal zero, and federal debt will stop growing. Credit will flow thus: central bank to a commercial bank owned by the federal government, and then to private industry. We will be able to finance construction of modern new cities, bullet-speed trains, and everything this country needs at low interest rates. New money, as ever, will be created with new debt. The new money created by the commercial bank owned by the federal government will go entirely into investment, and not consumption. If the United States finds itself in a do-or-die arms race, we will be able to do it with zero interest loans to our defense and related industries.

The world economy is growing, and it needs more and more dollars because most international trade is done with dollars. It means that the United States must have a sizable trade deficit. In other words, we have to buy from the world more than we sell, but it does not mean that we should buy anything from China. Gradually, our economy must disentangle itself from China. How large should our global trade deficit be? There are a few factors to consider. First, we should not become an agricultural province of the world. Just the opposite. If the world economy needs more dollars, we can gradually increase money supply so that a part of it will be used to buy more from the world, mostly raw materials and agricultural products, not the other way around. Is it really necessary for this superpower to manufacture sugar or fatten pigs? We can buy all the sugar that we need from India and Brazil. We can buy all the pork that we eat from Vietnam and a few other countries. Instead, we should subsidize our high-tech manufacturing with zero-interest loans. Otherwise, we have no chance against China.

The second factor is related to the exchange rates of currencies. Lower exchange rates mean cheaper currency; it allows exporters to sell their goods at lower prices. Exchange rates are influenced by a number of factors.

First, is purchasing power. The higher the purchasing power the higher is usually the exchange rate of the currency.

Second, is real interest rates (nominal interest rates minus expected rate of inflation). The rate of real interest is itself affected by the credit rating of the borrower. A country with a strong credit rating like the United States should be able to sell its government bonds at lower rates of real interest than a country with a weak credit rating like Greece. But let's take a look. It is the end of September, 2019. A 10-yr Treasury bond is traded at approximately the same real interest rate as a Greek 10-yr government bond. That is because of the third factor affecting the exchange rate. The European Central Bank prints euros and buys government bonds of individual countries of the European Union at inflated prices.

The fourth factor affecting the exchange rates is financial speculation. Major currencies are traded as currency futures. The big Wall Street firms have the ability to manipulate the prices of currencies. When they buy or sell large amounts of anything, it affects prices. The smaller fish then tries to get a piece of the action, and the price moves further while the big fish earns a profit selling into the boom and buying in the bust. Because there are many thousands of financial speculators, they amplify the market moves in both directions. When too many traders buy, the price moves up too much, and when they eventually start selling, there is a potential for a bust. This is how markets for all speculative goods function.

And finally, last but not least, the fifth factor. Printing money to buy government debt moves bond prices up, interest rates down, and the price of that currency down (in terms of other currencies). The proposed modified Keynesianism will be increasing the money supply, inflation will be elevated but only in the short term. In the long term both the standard of living and quality of life will increase. This means that the purchasing power of the currency will not get weaker, and the exchange rates will be stable. Unless, of course, the currency futures speculators mess up everything for the single purpose of making money. That is why any country contemplating the use of modified Keynesianism should first stop the trading of its currency in the futures market. Otherwise, the financial parasites will blame wild price distortions on modified Keynesianism.

Modified Keynesianism will also carry important implications for investment and savings (I—S) as well as for mobility of the financial capital in the world economy. The subject of the mobility of financial capital is an important issue both for economic theory and as a practical matter affecting many countries. For example, the Feldstein-Horioka puzzle deals with why levels of investment and saving are correlated across countries.

This is a very interesting problem in macroeconomics and international finance, which was first documented by Martin Feldstein and Charles Horioka in a 1980s paper. But first let's discuss a few minor issues we need to understand before we turn to the mobility of capital.

As we already know, new money is created with new debt when banks make loans. Some of the new money is spent for consumption; to pay for a vacation, for example. Some of the new money is invested. At any rate, all the new money spent always ends up in someone's pocket or bank account, increasing monetary savings. Because your spending increases my savings, they are always equal in any one transaction. As each dollar changes hands, spending in the economy increases as a result of each transaction. But what about savings? Money supply does not increase, so monetary savings in the economy do not increase. Total monetary savings is equal to the total money supply.

As we see, some of the new money is invested, but that is not the total investment. When money circulates in the economy, businesses receive money as income. Businesses spend a part of that income to expand or otherwise to improve the business. Both spending and investing are a perpetual process.

There are two types of capital. Real capital includes land, buildings, machinery, etc. Financial capital includes stocks, bonds, and money.

Now we can take a look at the Feldstein-Horioka puzzle. Financial markets can rapidly divert financial capital from one country to another. One could expect that savings would be diverted from wherever they occur to where the best investment opportunities are by agents seeking to maximize returns. According to this reasoning, the levels of investment and saving should not be correlated across countries. However, Feldstein and Horioka (1980) found that this is not the case and that most incremental saving is in fact invested in the country in which it occurs. The puzzle is to try to understand why this should be the case.

In 2016, Nicholas Ford and Charles Horioka proposed a solution to the puzzle. The short version of the argument is that when financial capital moves to another country that has a different currency, the two currencies are exchanged and invested in opposite directions. After the exchange, American investors will invest the Japanese yen in Japan, and the Japanese investor will invest American dollars in the U.S. As a result, there is no net transfer of capital between the countries.

Agreed, but this is the right answer to the wrong question. Net transfer of capital between countries is not relevant to the original question which was, in simple words, why do domestic savings overwhelmingly finance domestic investment? In other words, if American investors were to finance $10 trillion worth of investment in Japan, and Japanese investors were to finance $10 trillion worth of investment in Germany, and German investors were to finance $10 trillion worth in America, then capital mobility would be apparent to everyone and this puzzle would not even exist, even though there is no net transfer of capital between the three countries. Which means that the proposed solution is totally wrong. The presence or absence of the net transfer of money is not relevant for the following reasons:

First, we should challenge the very notion that when one currency is exchanged for the equivalent amount of another currency, both currencies will be invested. That is not always the case. For example, an American exchanged $10,000 for euros to take a vacation in Europe. The American will spend euros for consumption, but the European might invest the dollars in American Treasures. This example illustrates the fact that money always flows in opposite directions, but some of it might be spent for consumption, and not for investment.

The second reason is that the central banks of many countries often print local currencies and exchange them for dollars. The dollars are kept in the reserves of the central banks. Whoever was the counter-party in such transactions will receive the local currency to invest or to spend for consumption.

As we see from these examples, there is no net transfer of money, it flows in opposite directions, but amounts invested are not necessarily equal. That is why it is possible that investment money goes in one direction, and consumption money goes in the opposite direction, but it still does not explain the original question.

We should note that China is building hundreds of infrastructure projects around the world but has none of the problems associated with exchange of currencies. A country in Africa needs to build something, be that a railroad, a power station, or whatever. Chinese companies build the project, often with

Chinese labor. The African country has a bill to pay for the job well done. No currency exchanges, no puzzles. Keep it simple. The payment is in green dollars.

The IMF should take the same approach. At the present time the IMF makes loans to poor countries in dollars. The government of the poor country will then exchange the dollars for the local currency. Often the central bank of the poor country will print local currency and buy dollars. The government spends local money, but has to pay the debt in dollars. Look what happened to Argentina. Bankrupt again.

If poor countries start using modified Keynesian theory, they will not need to borrow so much in foreign currencies. Most of their expenditure is in local money, and they should print local currency to make loans and finance domestic investment.

If many countries start using modified Keynesianism, what will happen to the mobility of the financial capital in the world economy? The need for foreign investment will be drastically reduced, and it will be good for the world economy. Actually, only investment to create new wealth—factories, infrastructure, etc.—should be allowed. Financial investments to pump and dump financial assets like stocks and bonds should be taxed heavily, as they leave behind only misery and devastation.

Now back to the puzzle. Why is most of the domestic investment financed with domestic savings? Let's take a look where the money for investment usually comes from. Business firms use the following sources of financing their investments: first, internal funds that originate in profits. Second, equity financing which means using shares of stock. Third, debt financing by using various debt instruments like bonds, promissory notes, etc. Fourth, when capital markets are not an option, especially for small companies, just borrowing from your friendly banker. These, in a nutshell, are the main sources of investment funds, and all these sources favor local knowledge of local business. Would you invest in a gold mine in a faraway land? Mark Twain gave us a good definition of a gold mine: a hole in the ground and a liar on the top. That definition is probably the best argument against investing in deep holes located in faraway lands.

Most rules have exceptions, of course. People like gambling, and the financial markets of the world provide the same rush of adrenaline to compulsive financial gamblers as casinos of Las Vegas. The financial casinos are full of smart computers, and they are programmed to separate you from your money. You will fall deep into the proverbial hole, and the liar will stay at the top.

At the time of my writing, 2019 is coming to an end. Globalization and the great relocation continue. The allure of getting rich by exploiting cheap labor is too great. Regardless of what happens in the future, China will have gained the most from globalization; the United States will be the biggest loser. The amount of technological knowledge transferred in exchange for elusive promises is too great. Empires make such asinine blunders maybe only once in a thousand years, and most do not survive. China is the only exception.

For the last two centuries, political discourse in Russia always included two great questions: "Who is to blame?" and, "What should we do?" In our current predicament, we should blame those economists who advocate free markets and globalization. What should we do? Modified Keynesian theory. Will it help? Only time will tell.

SLOW DEATH BY GLOBALIZATION

Imagine for a moment that during the Industrial Revolution all factories were relocated from England to China in search of cheaper labor. Which country would become the world power in the next century?

The development of classical economics started at the same time as the Industrial Revolution. Classical economists, most of them British, advocated free market and free trade, but none of them recommended relocating production to another country where labor was cheaper. What was it that classical economists did not understand about the benefits of globalization?

There is a very fine line between economic issues and political issues. The whole world is facing many economic problems—poverty, unemployment, low economic growth, economic instability, rising economic inequality, overpopulation in many parts of the world, pollution, etc. All economic issues represent political problems for governments of the world. This book describes and explains the most important fundamental problems in economics as related to practical economic policies.

Most economists reduce their vision of economics to a set of equations and statistical research, but that approach is not adequate. Growing up in the former Soviet Union, the author of this book had an opportunity to watch the train wreck of the Soviet economy in slow motion. There were no capitalists to exploit workers, free education, free healthcare, free housing (after waiting ten or fifteen years in line). How did the government pay for all that free stuff? You buy food, clothing, shoes, and everything else at hugely inflated prices. If the government paid a total of one ruble for production and distribution of an item, you would pay ten rubles. That is how the government paid for free education, healthcare, and housing, as well as an arms race with America. At some point people discovered that the profit margin was huge. Management at all levels of production started to steal from the government, from production of cotton and leather to distribution in retail stores.

There was also a very large distortion of prices. The price of delicious rye bread was so low that the population of villages and small towns were fattening piglets with it. The cost of production and distribution of rye bread was probably five times higher than the selling price. The result was that millions of people in the Soviet Union were working to produce millions of tons of delicious rye bread to feed pigs. It was a tremendous waste of labor.

When Ronald Reagan started his "Star Wars" arms race, the whole economic system of Soviet Union collapsed. The interesting thing is that economists in the West did not see the coming economic collapse, and most of those on the left simply could not see it coming. The moral of this little story is that equations and statistics are important (of course), but it is even more important to see the big picture, the whole economic mechanism, the nuts and bolts, and where and in which direction the whole thing is moving. When in doubt, do not assume anything. Check the simplest possibilities first. That is the first rule of diagnostics, and it brings us back to the process of globalization.

What is globalization? How does it work, and does it work for our benefit? Most people assume that globalization means free market and free trade. That is what classical economists advocated for, right? But no, none of them recommended the relocation of production from Britain to countries with low-cost labor. Later in the book we will discuss why technological progress and international trade worked so well for Britain. This is not just an academic question to satisfy intellectual curiosity about a process that started two and a half centuries ago. The whole history of mankind is full of examples of great Empires that no longer exist. The latest one being the Soviet Union which was destroyed by economic mismanagement, with a good push from Ronald Reagan. We have to make sure that a misunderstanding of the process of globalization will not cause the decline and fall of this great republic and civilization—the end of the American Century.

Economic instability is a fascinating topic. In the history of the United States there were quite a few economic depressions. The last one, the Great Depression, started in 1929. After the Second World War economic downturns that were not severe enough to qualify as a depression and may or may not have included an economic recession, have taken place every ten years, plus or minus a year or two. Economic downturns have taken place around 1950, 1960, 1970, 1980, 1990, 2000, and 2010 (started in 2007). The next one is "scheduled" for around 2020. Let's hope that it will be a garden variety downturn, but not an economic depression. Why is the author concerned? There is a full explanation later in this book, but here is a short story that is, well, depressing and indicative of the problems before us.

Classical economists generally held that economic depression did not require governmental intervention because the economy would correct itself. Then the Great Depression started in 1929, the economy was getting worse all the time, and it was not correcting itself. In 1932, four years before John Maynard Keynes published his General Theory, Irving Fisher, professor of economics at Yale University, published his classic book *Booms and Depressions*. Irving Fisher explained very clearly how liquidation of debt may start a vicious debt-liquidation spiral, when the economic depression feeds on itself. When commercial banks, for whatever reason, start collecting debt without making new loans, it causes currency contraction, or, in other words, less money in circulation. Decades later, Milton Friedman "discovered" that lower money supply caused the Great Depression. His assertion that the Federal Reserve could prevent the greatest depression is flatly wrong and misleading because at that point our monetary system was based on gold standard, and the Fed did not have a legal right just to print paper currency and to make loans to commercial banks. Irving Fisher explained that currency contraction, or a lower amount of money in circulation, causes lower demand and lower prices. Four years later, John Maynard Keynes published his General Theory, in which he detailed his "discovery" that low aggregate demand was the main problem of the depressed economy. He was wrong. The main problem was the monetary system based on the gold standard, and liquidation of debt was spiraling out of control, as Irving Fisher explained. To argue that either money supply is more important than aggregated demand (monetary theory) or vice versa (Keynesianism) is intellectually dishonest. Money supply and aggregate demand are like two sides of the same coin. Both ideas have been "borrowed" from Irving Fisher without any compensation. Each of the two ideas have been used as a cornerstone to build a new school of economic thought, but in reality, both were just creative marketing bastardizations of Irving Fisher's theory.

Why is it important for the world to know Irving Fisher's theory? There are at least two very compelling reasons. The first reason is that both schools of economic thought present a distorted and misleading version of Irving Fisher's theory without giving him a credit. It looks very much like shameless plagiarism.

The second reason is that, for some strange reason, Irving Fisher's theory has been actually banned, and was replaced by misleading theories at the time when the world needs it more than ever. There is a strong possibility that the next economic downturn will become an economic depression. Our economy might get sucked into a debt-deflation spiral while economists argue about money supply, demand, and velocity of money. Neither monetarism nor Keynesian economics will be able to offer an effective economic policy, because falling money supply and demand are just symptoms of the same disease, and not the real causes. The disease—and the root of the problem—is liquidation of debt.

An argument can be made that the Fed has a printing press and a helicopter to drop bags of currency and increase the reserves of commercial banks, so that they can make loans against those reserves. Every loan will increase the money supply by the amount of the loan, and will increase demand because more money will be chasing the goods. Why would it not work to stop the economic depression? This is a good question, and the answer requires telling a little story, the story mentioned above.

In 1933 Congress enacted the Banking Act, also known as Glass-Steagall Act. The principal author of the bill was Senator Carter Glass, an expert on monetary policy, who in 1913, in the House of Representatives, sponsored legislation that established the

Federal Reserve System. The Banking Act was made into law because it was recognized that commercial banks had a conflict of interest. On one hand, the banks were supposed to make loans to the economy to keep it strong. On the other hand, they would rather make loans to investment banks to buy assets at very depressed prices. The Banking Act of 1933 prohibited commercial banks from owning both investment banks and insurance companies. Senator Glass was aiming to eliminate incentives for commercial banks to choke the economy into depression and to buy assets for pennies on the dollar.

Fast forward to 1999. President Clinton, the Fed chairman Alan Greenspan, and Congress enacted legislation that allowed commercial banks to again own investment banks and insurance companies. Eight years later, in 2007, the financial crisis hit, and big banks bought all the major brokerage houses on Wall Street. It looks like ducks are being put into a row. The big banks again have both the incentive and the means to choke the economy, to make loans to investment companies they own, and to make a killing. Who could resist such a temptation? With the Glass-Steagall Act dead in the water, American economy looks very much like a sitting duck.

What might trigger the start of the debt-liquidation spiral? Almost anything. There are factors that cause economic downturns every ten years, plus or minus a year or two. Generally, the American economy depends on bank credit, as well as loans from insurance companies (construction loans, for example). The more loans the economy gets from commercial banks and insurance companies, the more both money supply and aggregate demand increase, and the stronger the economy becomes. When financial institutions have already used up all their reserves for making new loans, or the economy is already mired in debt, or both, then the banks start collecting debt, but make fewer loans. Aggregate demand and monetary supply decrease, and the economy enters a downturn. It is safe to say that instability of credit is the main cause of economic instability. If big banks decide to continue liquidating debt, the economy will be sucked into a debt-liquidation spiral, and the next ordinary decennial economic downturn will become an economic depression.

There are also other factors that contribute to economic instability. Issues in microeconomics—those that affect individual companies—are important enough to affect the whole economy. For example, the top management of publicly traded companies usually have stock options as part of the total compensation. The higher the company's stock prices go, the more money the top management makes. There are incentives to cook the books by understating expenses (depreciation, loss of value of capital assets like plants and equipment, for example) and overstating profits, which increases stock prices. Very many public companies practice this kind of "earnings management," but sooner or later expenses must be recognized and accounted for. That is when earnings take a hit, and it happens every ten years or so. As earnings are reduced, stock prices plunge, consumer confidence comes tumbling down and people spend less money which means that demand goes down, and the economy enters a downturn.

If our economy gets sucked into a debt-liquidation spiral, which school of economics is capable of offering an effective economic policy for stopping and reversing economic destruction? The easiest way to fight economic depression is to do nothing. That is exactly what rational expectations theory suggests we do. Seriously. We will take a look at their arguments later in the book just to demonstrate that they are wrong on every important point except one. If we do nothing, big banks will keep the liquidation of debt going: the economic depression will feed on itself; the big banks will keep making loans to their investment banks and insurance companies to buy assets at very depressed prices; it will last five or ten or twenty years. But sooner or later the banks will decide that enough is enough. The banks will start making loans to the real economy, and the economy will correct itself in the long run, but only after bankers buy everything in sight, pennies on the dollar. If we accept the rational expectations theory, the logical conclusion would be that the Great Depression should have been allowed to run its course, without any government interference, for five or ten or twenty years, until bankers were done with their business of buying assets at very depressed prices. Senator Glass, according to this logic, was not supposed to author the Glass-Steagall Act. The theory of rational expectations is the most delusional of all economic theories, unless, of course, their academic activity is sponsored and financed by bankers, which is much more likely than the possibility that the whole bunch of economists simply lost their minds.

Monetarism offers a much better approach to economic problems. Monetarism is soothing and comforting: just keep the money supply steady. The main problem with this approach is that a steady and moderate increase in money supply cannot guarantee economic stability. For example, the financial crisis started in 2007 after several years of very loose activities in the real estate market. In those years money supply was increasing very steadily and moderately, but banks were prequalifying millions of potential home buyers. And what happens when millions of people start searching for homes? Prices went up strongly even though artificial demand was not caused by an increase in money supply.

Here is another example: When stock prices go up, people feel wealthier, they spend more money, and the economy improves. When the stock market goes down, the process goes in reverse. At the present time, in May of 2018, the stock market is near record highs. A strong correction downward might serve as a trigger for an economic downturn, and as soon as it starts anything is possible. The bottom line here is that monetarist theory rejects an active role for the government, but has no mechanism to save a tumbling economy. When discussing economic theories, we should understand how a certain theory keeps the economy stable, with low unemployment, low inflation, and maximum output. Of course, we know that those goals are very often conflicting, and choices in economic policies involve trade-offs. The trick is to find the optimal solution, the least bad among bad choices, and every school of economics has its own perspective on how to keep the economy in the best possible condition. But what should we do when the economy enters a downturn? In a globalized world we cannot be sure that our economy will stay strong. We need to have effective means to fight an economic depression, so we should evaluate economic theories on the basis of what exactly they advocate doing in both good times and bad times. The theory of rational expectations and the monetarist theory reject an active role for the government, so they are useless when the economy is crushing down.

Now let's take a quick look at supply-side economics. How does it address good times and bad times? But first, let's recall what we know about supply. Aggregate supply is what we produce and offer for sale. If we produce less, we will consume less, so supply-side is very important in good times. The question is how to increase, and keep increasing, aggregate supply. I know only one method of increasing supply effectively. A bank makes a loan to build, but not to buy, a building or any other desirable capital asset. A loan to build a new building will increase the supply of real estate and will increase the wealth of the country. A loan to buy an existing asset will only increase demand, but not wealth of the country. To finance an increase in supply is clearly better for the economy.

Are the supply-siders advocating the financing of an increase in supply? No, they are advocating a reduction of taxation, which will cause a number of benefits to take place. Consumers and businesses will pay lower taxes, they will have more money left over to spend and to invest, and this increased demand (more after-tax money is nothing but demand) will increase supply and our total output. Increased demand creates its own supply. This idea should sound familiar. If we peel off a couple of layers of this onion, we will find Keynes inside. They agree that stimulation of the economy by increased demand works every time in the short run, and in the long run all monetarists are dead. Which brings us to the next school of economic thought: the Keynesians.

Both the supply-side and the Keynesian schools are very skeptical about the effectiveness of economic policies advocated by monetarists, and they have very good reasons for their skepticism. Looking at the years of real estate mania before the 2007 financial crisis through a monetarist's magnifying glass, there was nothing disturbing. The wild speculation in real estate was flying below monetarist's radar because the monetary aggregates were increasing at a very optimal rate. The enormous artificial demand was not visible because it was created not by loans to buy real estate, but by promises of bankers to home buyers—millions of them—to give them loans to buy homes, and no live red-blooded monetarist will ever agree that a mere promise to give a loan could possibly affect the real economy. The point here is not that monetary aggregates do not matter; of course, they do. The point, rather, is that even with steady monetary aggregates, when nothing on the surface is making waves, a tsunami may move invisibly until it hits the shore with devastating effect. And what exactly would cause the creation of such a wave, one that can travel under the surface a very long distance, evading detection for a prolonged period of time?

Irving Fisher did not, to my knowledge, use this metaphor, but in his theory accumulation of debt stands for the tsunami. The more debt is accumulated the bigger the invisible wave is, and the bigger the potential for devastation, if and when liquidation of debt starts. Does this mean that we should not accumulate debt? No, that is impossible. Every loan from the bank increases money supply—and the size of the tsunami, because a bank loan is debt to be paid. Accumulation of debt creates prosperity, especially if the debt is productive (for example, a loan to build a new house as opposed to a loan to buy an existing home). Irving Fisher differentiated between productive and unproductive debts. Liquidation of debt, like a tsunami hitting the shore, devastates the economy. Now, why did we not discuss this tsunami earlier, in monetarism? Because monetarism has no active role for the government to play, and no tools to fight liquidation of debt if the economy gets sucked into a debt-liquidation spiral. Milton Friedman argued that monetary policy works with "long and variable lags," so it would not smooth out the business cycle. Actually, Friedman was right. The Fed does not have adequate control over American economy.

Let's take a look how the Fed operates. With one hand, the treasury prints Treasury Securities and sells them. With another hand, the treasury prints currency and sells it to the Fed for the cost of printing, which is very low. From time to time the Fed buys Treasuries on the open market and pays with currency received from the treasury for the cost of printing. There's nothing wrong with this practice because the dollar is the chief reserve currency of the world, and the growing world economy requires more dollars. The point here is that the Fed has the ability to buy an unlimited number of Treasuries and inject an unlimited amount of money into the economy. The problem is that most of what the Fed pays for the Treasuries goes to big commercial banks and becomes a part of their reserves. If the banks decide to make loans against those reserves quickly, the economy will recover quickly. If the big banks decide to delay lending, there will be "long and variable lags," as Friedman put it.

The Fed may apply pressure, but the big banks decide when to increase lending. If our economy gets knocked down into an economic depression, the Fed has no control of the economy. If the big banks decide that they would rather make loans to the investment banks they own, the depression will last many years, until they are finished buying everything they can.

It is clear that monetarism has no tools to keep the economy strong either in good times or in bad times. Supply-siders aim to stimulate demand, but at the cost of increasing budget deficits and government debt. They should be considered Keynesians, but kind of a light version, without any tools to combat an economic depression. Supply side Keynesianism will work every time until it doesn't. At some point banks will start collecting more debt than they loan out. Both money supply and demand will start dropping.

What can we do when liquidation of debt picks up speed? First, we need the new Glass-Steagall Act as soon as possible. If we do not succeed, we need tools to increase demand effectively and quickly. This means many billions of dollars in loans to build everything this nation needs. Housing is not affordable; we need to increase the supply of housing. We can make loans to real estate developers to build modern new cities with modern public transportation. City blocks should be about one square mile each. High-rise apartment buildings should be located at the perimeter, close to the public transportation, which will be available at all four sides of any block. In the middle of a residential city block there will be most of what people need, within walking distance —schools, medical clinics, after school facilities, and a shopping center. Later in the book there is a more detailed description of a residential city block. Since four sides of one square mile are four miles in total, around ten thousand apartments can be built at the perimeter. If one apartment is around $300,000 in construction costs, then 10,000 apartments need $3 billion. Add restaurants, stores, etc. on the ground floor of the buildings; as well as schools, medical centers, and shopping centers, etc. in the middle of the residential block. The total cost of construction of just one residential block will be at least $4 billion. Big banks won't want to finance such projects and create productive jobs, especially when the whole economy is in a depression.

In the 1930s Keynes thought that the government should borrow money and create jobs. At that point our monetary system was based on the gold standard, and the government could not print paper currency. Today we don't have a gold standard. We can create a commercial bank owned by the federal government. The commercial bank will not be taking deposits from the public. Instead, the commercial bank will borrow money (reserves) straight from the Fed and make multi-billion-dollar construction loans. Construction will take a few years; the real estate developer will sell the real estate and will pay back his loan to the commercial bank, which will pay back its own loan to the Fed. America needs to build at least one million new apartments every year. If the cost of one block is at least $4 billion, the total cost of construction will be $300 billion. We need to start construction of such cities as soon as possible. If and when an economic depression hits, we will be able to expand quickly. Are there any negative aspects in this proposal to create a government-owned commercial bank, to print currency and to make construction loans? Most certainly. But this is the least bad solution among many other bad solutions.

Some economists will point out that the Fed will have to print billions of dollars and make loans to a government-owned commercial bank, but the Fed does not usually make loans, except in extraordinary situations like the 1987 stock market crash. Well, if the Fed can make loans to financial speculators to support financial markets by buying stocks at low prices, why not make loans to build modern new cities and create millions of jobs? During an economic depression it would be the best strategy because it will increase both money supply and aggregate demand very quickly and effectively. The problem is that it will be impossible to start construction on a large scale in the middle of nowhere. We need to start construction of several new cities, so that if a city already has a dozen of blocks, construction of another dozen can be started on all four sides of the city.

How many jobs will be created? If the construction cost of one apartment is about $300,000 and an average worker earns about $30,000 per year, then construction of one apartment will create ten jobs in construction and construction materials industries. Construction of one million apartments will create ten million jobs. If we add what will be built in the middle of the blocks—schools, medical, shopping, etc., —it will be a few millions more.

On the other hand, some construction materials will be imported, so we will be able to support the world economy if the economic depression is worldwide. But the most important thing is perception. If we make it known that we can print and loan whatever amount of money is needed to build a million of apartments and to create ten million jobs, bankers will know that they will not be able to throw us into an economic depression, so they will not even try.

There are two types of deposits. There are customers who opened savings accounts and deposited their own money. It is their money, and they have a right to withdraw cash. The second type of deposits are those deposits that were generated by banks when customers borrowed money. Banks can raid their customers who are trying to raid banks. Irving Fisher explained: "In fact, banks find themselves engaged in a race for "liquidity." They begin to call their loans; but by calling loans, they help further to extinguish deposit currency... This hoarding of money by banks has a magnified effect on deposit currency; for every dollar of reserve in a bank may support, say, ten dollars of loans," (*Booms and Depressions*, page 51). The problem, as we see, is that both sides can destabilize the system. The customers can raid the banks to withdraw cash. The banks can raid their customers and call their loans, which means that the loans must be paid back in a short period of time. It starts a vicious cycle of liquidation of debt, when assets are sold to pay back loans, which causes lower prices, which makes production not profitable, which causes business closures, more liquidation of debt, still lower prices, lower demand, lower money supply, and so on into a debt-liquidation spiral.

So, what can be done to improve the stability of the world's financial system? It must be clear that the banks should not raid their customers and start the debt-liquidation spiral. Let's take a look at the main idea of the Basel III Accord. A Google search will give you a pretty good understanding of the Basel III agreement. It requires improving the stability of the world's financial system by increasing the capital of the most important banks. By "capital" they do not mean banks' own capital. Banks' own capital means what shareholders own, and it can be increased only by selling additional shares of stock to investors. If the world's biggest banks sell billions of new shares of stock, it will relocate money from smaller banks to the big ones. This trick will not improve the world's financial system as a whole. Big banks will have more capital of their own, but smaller ones will lose an equal amount of their reserves. Can we increase reserves of big banks? Yes, just increase interest rates on your deposits, and people will start closing their deposits in smaller banks and moving them to the big banks. That is one way to increase the bank reserves in big banks, but this tactic will start a bidding war for deposits, and a system-wide increase of interest rates. There is a second possibility, which is much worse.

Let's use the same example. A banking system with $1 million in bank reserves and $10 million in deposits. What will happen if minimum reserve requirements increase from 10% to 15%? Of course, big banks will increase interest rates to attract deposits, but if that does not work, there will be only a nuclear option left —to reduce the amount of deposits. Supposed, for simplicity, that the minimum reserve requirements increased for the whole banking system, which has $1 million in reserves, from 10% to 15%. It means that $1 million in reserves must be equal to 15% of deposits. $1 million=15% of deposits. 1%= $1 million divided by 15, and 100% of deposits is 100 times more. $1,000,000/15 multiplied by 100=$6,666,666. As we see, an increase in minimum reserve requirements from 10% to 15% may result in a decrease in the total deposits from $10 million to $6,666,666 which is a 33% reduction.

We can assume that because only the big banks will be required to increase their capital, the total amount of deposits will drop by only 20%. Well, Irving Fisher provides this statistic: "From 1929 to 1932, judging by the records of the Federal Reserve member banks, deposit currency had lost 21 per cent of its volume and 61 per cent of its velocity; the remaining efficiency for business purposes being only 31 per cent of its efficiency in 1929. The growth of pessimism is sufficiently indicated by this record," (*Booms and Depressions*, page 117). As we see, deposits lost only 21%, and it was enough to throw the economy into the Great Depression. If the Basel bankers are successful in forcing the big banks to increase their "capital" significantly, which is the stipulation of the Basel III Accord, the whole world economy will be pushed into depression.

Now, what can we do to really improve the stability of the world's financial system? There are quite a few things we should do. First, of course, we need a new Glass-Steagall Act to eliminate incentives for bankers to push the economy into a depression.

Also, we need to increase the minimum reserve requirements very gradually and slowly. Here is a way to do it without hurting the economy.

It must be done not by banks raiding customers, but by increasing the reserves without any reduction in deposits. Using our example, how can we increase total reserves of the banking system from 10% of deposits to 15%? Let's recall the proposal to print currency and to make construction loans to build modern new cities. With jobs coming back from China, there will be not only residential blocks, but also industrial blocks. Billions and billions of new printed currencies will be needed to support new loans and deposits. This new currency will increase the total reserves of the banking system. At that time the Fed can increase the minimum reserve requirements by, maybe, one quarter of 1%, from, say, 10% of deposits to 10. 25% of deposits. The banks will have more green dollars in reserve, both as nominal amounts and as percentage of deposits. The "capital" requirements of Basel bankers will be met. As long as we continue to increase the amount of new loans with newly printed currency, the total reserves of the banking system will increase. But construction loans are only for a few years. As new real estate is built and sold, loans will be paid back, and every loan paid back reduces money supply. You borrow a hundred dollars from a bank; money supply is increased by a hundred dollars. You pay back $110 (with interest), and money supply is decreased by $110. Now, what will happen if everything has already been built, and most of the loans have been paid back? Then money supply will decline catastrophically. If we ever have such a problem, there is only one solution. We will have to increase money supply not with loans, but permanently. Just print currency, give it to the government, which is very good at spending, and this way we can inject reserves into the banking system permanently. Hopefully, we will be able to pay for construction of high-speed railroads, and aqueducts from Northern to Southern California, and many other projects.

The science of economics has a problem. The basic mechanism of any economy is very simple. Economists have a moral obligation to explain to the world how to improve the lives of the people, especially in poor countries. At the present time the accepted wisdom is that developing countries should borrow money from rich countries and invest that money in all kinds of projects, most of which are of questionable value. This practice rarely works well for anyone involved, except, of course, for investment bankers who unload overpriced debt instruments of poor countries to uninformed investors.

Just a couple of years ago, for example, Argentina borrowed a huge amount of money on the world financial market. Now, how does one spend dollars in a country where the local currency is a peso? To buy things on the world market you can use borrowed dollars, but to pay for something inside Argentina you have to exchange borrowed dollars for pesos, which increases demand for pesos (in terms of other currencies) to an artificially high level. But sooner or later the process of exchange of borrowed dollars comes to an end, and then the bubble bursts. As the price of the peso started to fall to a more reasonable level, where it reflected its purchasing power, the central bank intervened to support the inflated price of the peso. Normally, the central bank is supposed to sell dollars in exchange for pesos. Obviously, they no longer have enough dollars to sell. *The Economist* (May 25th, 2018) just reported, "Argentina's central bank raised its benchmark interest rate from 27.25% to 30.25% in an effort to shore up the peso, which has taken a battering in currency markets amid worries about stubbornly high inflation."

It is tempting to say that to increase interest rates to 30% is pure insanity, but it is not, and it is not ignorance either. International bankers have attended some of the best business schools. They know what they are doing, just like Basel bankers know what they are doing. There is only one reasonable explanation—greed, corruption, and evil intent. That is why economists have a moral obligation to write economics textbooks in which instead of obscure concepts there will be a clear explanation of the nuts and bolts and the moving parts of the real economy's real workings.

With regard to Argentina, if the central bank prints local currency and makes loans to build whatever the country needs—housing, schools, hospitals, chicken farms, etc.—millions of jobs will be created, the wealth of the country will increase, and interest rates, even on long bonds, will be between 10% and 15%. Why? For two reasons. First, construction loans are only for a few years, and money will disappear as loans are paid back. So, in the long run inflation will be low. The second reason is that to finance infrastructure the government can issue long-term bonds, and whenever the price of bonds drops to around 15%, the central bank can print pesos and buy the bonds in order to push price up and interest rates down. Argentina does not really need to borrow money in a foreign currency. Argentina can print its own pesos, and make productive loans, and increase the wealth of the country, and inflation will stay low, and there will be no reason whatsoever for the short-term interest rate to go higher than, say, 5%.

Most of the poor countries of the world do not really need to follow the rich countries' patterns of development, with sprawling suburbs and a high rate of individual car ownership. Poor countries can print their own currency and make loans to build modern new cities where most of everything is inside the city block: schools, child care, medical clinics, shopping centers, etc. Poor countries will not need to build hundreds of thousands of miles of roads and highways, long lines of infrastructure (water, sewage, electricity, etc.) and most individuals will not even need to own cars. People in poor countries need, first of all, basic necessities—housing, food, and clothing; car ownership is non-essential. Urban sprawl makes everyone poorer. When a country is covering huge areas with single-family houses and roads and streets leading to those houses, that country is losing not only open space, but also agricultural land.

It so happened that today, May 8th 2018, I watched the debate of the leading candidates in the race for governor of California. It is clear that immigrants are a very powerful constituency. Sooner or later California's borders will be open for millions of people to come every year. California is already a sanctuary state, and anyone who wants to overstay their visa and remain in the U.S. illegally will be safe from deportation here.

One way or another, the population of California could increase up to 100 million people by the end of the century. In order to save the environment, the open space, and agricultural land we need to start construction of modern new cities immediately. If we destroy agricultural land, we will not be able to produce enough food for the population, and America will become as poor as any of those countries that have large populations but not enough agricultural land to feed their population. America is already moving in that direction.

The Democrat Party has very conflicting goals, at least as they are publicly stated. They want to help the poor, make housing affordable, and increase standard and quality of life in general. Democrats are against big oil because cars cause pollution, so those who are concerned about the environment and global warming tend to vote for Democrats. Now, here is the idea to build modern new cities with modern public transportation, where most people will not even need to own cars, and here is the full explanation how to finance construction of the modern cities, but the top Democrats are not interested.

My understanding is that the leadership of the Democrat Party cannot accept this idea for the following reasons. First, the poor tend to vote for Democrats, who promise to tax the rich and give the money to the poor. The more poverty there is, the more people will vote for Democrats. Construction of modern new cities will increase the supply of housing, will make it much more affordable, reduce poverty, and reduce the number of poor voters who support Democrats. The second reason is that the problems of environmental pollution and global warming will become less pressing, and the number of voters who are concerned about the environment will drop also. The leadership of the Democrat Party is very smart, very calculating. They do not want to shoot themselves in the foot. It is my hope that readers of this book will promote this idea on social services, and somehow, we will be able to force both major parties to reduce poverty in the United States.

At the present time not only are minimum wages going up, but all wages are increasing. Does it help the poor who rent an apartment? No, because people have more money to pay rent, and landlords are increasing rent payments. There is only one solution to help the poor and the middle class. Build modern new cities. The federal government owns about 50% of land in the western states. Sell some of that land to real estate developers at a very low price, but with the condition they build not single-family houses, but modern new cities. If the central bank makes construction loans with low interest rates, savings will be passed on to the buyers of apartments. People will be able to buy apartments at affordable prices. Mortgage payments represent forced savings. Finally, people will start saving for retirement.

There will be strong opposition from two groups: Democrats and bankers. Democrats will engage environmental organizations to oppose construction anywhere while inviting in more immigrants. This is logical and predictable—the more poverty the more Democrats. The top management of big banks will oppose the idea for different reasons. The construction of modern new cities will increase supply of affordable housing. House prices will drop. Mortgages will shrink as people borrow smaller amounts to buy apartments. Big banks' profits will suffer. The union of democrats and big banks will try to push back. Talking heads on TV will be telling us that America is a country of immigrants, and we should open our borders and invite billions of people from all over the world while restricting construction in order to save the environment. Bankers will engage economists who will be telling us that printing money caused hyperinflation in Germany, so we should not loan money to build modern cities. The only acceptable way to print money is the American way, when the Treasury Department with one hand prints treasury bonds, and with another hand prints green dollars and gives them to the Fed for the cost of printing to buy those Treasury bonds. We should expect a lot of brainwashing from Democrats and bankers, and especially from those who are Democrats and bankers.

The Pentagon predicts that by 2050 there will be wars all over the world for natural resources. The population of the world is growing rapidly, especially in Africa and Asia. As the world population grows, the degradation of the environment will only get worse. If the growing population of the world continues to destroy agricultural land, shortages of food will become much worse, and very soon. The world needs to slow the increase of population or build modern new cities.

Why is what is going on in Africa and Asia important for America? Because the United States is not immune to what is going on in the world. As the number of immigrants in the U.S. increases (and I am an immigrant myself), and millions become citizens of this country, they will vote—very democratically—to open the borders to refugees, and especially for their own relatives.

With the whole world on fire, the United States will be reduced to infighting between different races and ethnic groups. With so many assault weapons in the United States, what should we expect? Most of Mexico is already controlled by drug cartels, and the United States is moving in the same direction. China and Russia do not really need to destroy the U.S. America will destroy itself. What can be considered reasonable immigration policy? Allow well educated people from all over the world to come to the U.S., America needs people with brains. We should do everything possible to improve the world so that there will be fewer refugees, but America should drastically reduce the number of refugees. If we lose control of our borders, it will spell the end of American century.

WHAT IS WRONG WITH REPUBLICANS

The political spectrum of the United States can be visualized as a horizontal line, with extreme left at the left end of the line, and the extreme right at the right end. The extreme left advocates Marxist socialism which, in theory, offers more economic and political equality. Such a society would be very easy to create. Given that hundreds of thousands of college students are brainwashed every year in our liberal universities, why not give them an opportunity to build a society of their dreams in one of our liberal states? Our federal government should provide a large piece of land to lease for 99 years. Liberal foundations will provide financing to build Utopia, the new socialist city. Professors of political science will oversee the construction, and will serve as the first government of the city until the elections. This is the only way to find out whether Marxism contains any useful lessons for social organization or if it's all just hot air. Most of us already know the answer, but the extreme left should be given the opportunity to discover the objective reality of Marxist socialism for themselves.

The extreme right resides at the opposite end of the political spectrum. The right-wingers distrust any notion of government ownership, and they are right. Just one example: After the Second World War, both Great Britain and Japan were in bad shape. Japan embraced capitalism wholeheartedly, without reservation, and took advantage of the vast American market being open for Japan's exports. Great Britain, on the other hand, became infatuated with Marxism. The Labor party nationalized everything it could put their hands on, carried away by foolish affection for the charms of socialism. In just a few decades the results were obvious and easy to understand. Japan built an enviable high-tech industry and a very competitive economy in general. Great Britain, once a great empire, became a second-rate power. It should be obvious to anyone that the easiest way to dumb down any economy is to follow the shining path of socialism down that rat hole of nationalization.

Now let's ask a difficult question. If socialism is so debilitating, then why do the authors of this book advocate the establishment of a central bank and a commercial bank, both owned and controlled by the federal government? The short answer is, all means of production should be in private hands, as a rule. Exceptions only confirm the rule. There is no reason to keep the Federal Reserve System in private hands. The Fed must be owned and controlled by the federal government. The same applies to a commercial bank which will be needed to make loans to hundreds of S&P 500 companies if and when the next economic depression strikes. The central bank will need to keep at least $1 trillion in currency ready for distribution in case there is a run on the banks. If the public knows there is no shortage of cash, there will be no financial panic.

Republicans should accept that not everything should be in private hands. Local police, firefighters, K-12 schools, community colleges, community hospitals and medical centers: all these institutions can function perfectly well without being privately owned.

Statistics tell us wherever there are both public and private (charter) K-12 schools, students of charter schools invariably boast better academic performance. Does it prove that charter schools provide better education? No, in most cases that is an illusion. Statistical data does not explain that in public schools there are too many students who don't want to learn anything. Good students escape to charter schools; the best students get skimmed off the top. The rest stay behind to complain about bad schools. It is not schools that are bad; it is the students. Ask an average graduate of an inner-city high school to calculate 123% of 123 without a calculator. Most of them will give you a blank stare. Tell them that 1% of 123 is 123/100, and 123% is just 123 times bigger. Very few of them will understand this simple logic.

And what is the solution? To privatize all the public schools? No, the solution is to accept that not every student must get a high school diploma. Even the most high-tech economy needs dishwashers, burger flippers, and janitors. We cannot privatize everything.

Healthcare is a subject of much debate. The federal government can provide low interest construction loans to build community hospitals, but most communities should finance operating costs of their hospitals through local and state taxes. That is how "Medicare-for-all" should be implemented: build it, own it, and operate it. It's time to stop blaming the private sector for the lack of affordable healthcare. Community hospitals already provide free care to anyone who cannot pay their medical bills. It's time to make it official: we already have free hospital care for everyone through community hospitals.

Private health insurance? If anyone decides to buy private health insurance they can do so, this is a free country. The rich and the upper middle class will certainly use private hospitals and medical centers. There is no need to eliminate private health insurance. Most importantly, the healthcare problem will be solved, and Democrats will lose one of their winning issues. And that is why they will resist taking this advice. Republicans should get smart and help the Democrats to eliminate this issue.

Where should we start? Low interest construction loans from the central bank to build community hospitals and medical centers. Republicans should learn that the private sector cannot solve each and every problem. Governments, on all levels, can and should play an important role. One of the most important roles of the federal government should be providing low interest loans to projects of national importance through the central bank. Borrowing from the central bank to finance important projects will create millions of jobs. When completed, those projects will increase the production of goods and services. For example, the construction of an aqueduct from Northern California to the Central Valley will allow farmers to increase production of nuts, fruits, and vegetables. Construction of a high-speed railway will allow travelers to avoid flying in our overcrowded skies.

But the difficult part is how to pay the accumulated debt back. Well, the short answer is that if we borrow, say, $1 trillion from the central bank every year, we have to collect $1 trillion in additional taxes at some time in the future. As long as money is pumped into the economy, it can be pumped out as taxes and paid back to the central bank, so this borrowing will not increase inflation in the long run, but we will certainly increase our prosperity and quality of life.

Big banks, of course, will not like the idea of being cut out of the picture. Their economics departments will try to scare us with predictions of runaway inflation caused by the central bank printing money. The big banks will put talking heads on TV to advocate for the continuation of the current policies, but we should remember that big banks have no incentive to keep our economy stable. Their investment banks are ready to buy assets at low prices if and when the economic depression arrives.

Republicans should accept that the free market and no government intervention means that during an economic depression Wall Street foxes will be in charge of our economic hen house and if we allow it, feathers will fly. Low taxes and little regulation are good, only when the economy is good.

WHAT IS WRONG WITH DEMOCRATS

The agendas of political parties are always evolving. The latest example is President Donald Trump, who hijacked the Republican party and converted it from the party of the rich into the party of the middle class and the poor. How did he do it?

A few decades ago, Democrats were the party of the working class. Democrats were against globalization and free trade. They were proud protectionists, and all for tariffs intended to protect domestic industry from foreign competition. Then President Nixon offered to China a deal they could not refuse: access to the world market and huge investments in return for economic reforms. What was he thinking?

It was during the hottest part of the Cold War. Every year one country or another would succumb to Soviet propaganda which was promising liberty, equality, and fraternity just as soon as every one-goat-village makes that one goat communal property. Liberal professors of political science were predicting the end of capitalism. It was at that time when President Nixon decided to knock China out of the Communist bloc. Protectionist Democrats, naturally, resisted Nixon's economic partnership with China. Probably, it was the main reason why the obstructionists managed to force President Nixon to resign, but the China deal became a great success. Economic growth in China literally exploded. Soviet propaganda was demoralized. It was one of the great stories of the Cold War. Nixon's China strategy has demonstrated to the whole world that capitalism has advantages over Marxist socialism. President Nixon built the foundation for President Reagan to destroy the evil empire.

There were also costs associated with the China deal. Simple accounting logic dictated the closure of labor-intensive production in the U.S. and its relocation to China. Only the headquarters of companies would stay in the U.S. to manage the import of cheap Chinese goods.

Over a couple of decades Democrats became corrupt, both morally and intellectually. Many people discovered that they could get rich by closing factories in the U.S. and moving production to China, and not many people were understanding the dangers of this process of deindustrialization. Nixon's advisers most likely were expecting only labor-intensive industries to move to China, but this process of globalization has acquired momentum of its own. The intention might have been to move the production of toys, shoes, textiles, clothing, and other low-tech goods out of the U.S., with the understanding that China would buy capital goods—factory machinery and equipment—from the U.S. It was a very good plan—to buy low-tech goods from China and sell high-tech goods to China, but it did not work out. China now buys factory machinery and equipment from Germany, Japan, and some other countries, and all these countries benefit from globalization. And what does China buy from the U.S.? Mostly agricultural goods—corn, soybeans, pork bellies. . . Slowly but surely the United States is becoming an agricultural colony of China.

A quick look at economic history makes it clear that all colonial powers tried to import raw materials from their colonies and sell manufactured goods to those colonies. In trade with China the U.S. does it backwards. Before Mr. Trump was elected, the U.S. was on a mission to destroy itself through globalization and free trade. We got lucky, but our luck may not last long. Our allies—Britain, Germany, France—are understandably unhappy with President Trump. They want to export more goods to China. China needs to export more goods to the U.S., otherwise China will not have dollars to buy goods from Europe. Now everyone is blaming the U.S. for not continuing the suicide mission, and disrupting the happy world trade markets. Even *The Economist*, a very influential magazine published in the United Kingdom, is constantly blaming President Trump for the start of the trade war with China.

Are they really so dumb? No. They have their own economic interests. When the U.K. decided to leave the European Union, the E.U. made it clear that there will be no free trade between the E.U. and the U.K. Is this little Great Britain so harmful for the economy of the E.U.? The U.K. will not flood the E.U. with cheap goods like China does to the U.S. Then why not have free trade without protective tariffs?

The answer is very simple. Everyone is practicing protectionism, and everyone is blaming President Trump for protectionism. Everyone wants to protect their own economy, and everyone wants the U.S., to continue to self-destruct via free trade and globalization.

The Trans-Pacific Free Trade Agreement negotiated by President Obama would have been the final nail in the coffin of the American economy. Imagine for a minute a dozen countries exporting to the U.S. all kinds of goods without tariffs—and spending the dollars to buy goods from China where prices are much lower. This level of total incompetence at the very top level of the U.S. federal government is difficult to understand. Fortunately, President Trump killed the deal as soon as he took office.

Democrats want to promote democracy around the world. They believe it should be America's mission. But the world is looking at the U.S. and sees a total mess. In healthcare, litigation lawyers are consuming medical insurance companies; insurance companies are consuming hospitals and doctors, which, in turn, are consuming their patients. Patients are at the very bottom of this parasitic food chain, and that is why our healthcare system is so expensive and inefficient.

Democrats should propose building community hospitals and medical centers where litigation lawyers will not be able to extort so much money. But with 99% of litigation lawyers being Democrats and a major source of donations for political campaigns, we cannot expect Democrats to improve a system from which they benefit.

There is a small chance that President Trump will overcome his party's distrust for government solutions as opposed to solutions generated by private industry, and will propose the creation of a central bank owned by the federal government. It will allow for the financing of projects of national importance at low interest rates. As a presidential candidate, Mr. Trump single-handedly created an apostasy movement against the elitist policies of globalization and free trade. It is still possible that President Trump will become an apostle of change and an architect of a major reform of our financial system. The simple truth is that a central bank owned by the federal government has become an absolute necessity for the financial system of the United States. If neither Democrats nor Republicans start advocating for its creation, the voters of the U.S. should abandon both major political parties and create a new Social-Democrat political party.

At the present time the composition of the Democratic Party is a curious concoction of true believers and cynics. The whole ideological platform of Democrats is created by cynics who do not believe in their own propaganda, which is only for consumption of true believers who communicate mostly heart to heart, bypassing any brains. Call it a Democrat syndrome. There is a long list of policies used by Democrats for the sole purpose of agitating people, without any intention of solving the problems. Their permanent winning issues are economic inequality, poverty, and affordability of housing. These issues are interconnected, and require the creation of a central bank owned by the federal government.

Global warming is the new issue for which America is receiving primary blame, Republicans in particular. China and India, and many other countries burn record amounts of coal, but Democrats and the media disseminate news claiming that global warming is America's fault, and the whole world constantly repeats these alternative facts created by Democrats' propaganda machinations. Build modern new cities? Democrats are not interested. The world is overpopulated, and it is also one of the major factors contributing to global warming, but the Democrats are not interested in telling the truth.

In the 21st century sales of guns and ammunition have exploded. The reason? Most people will not say it loudly, but there is a strong feeling that the melting pot is melting, and the breakup will not be peaceful. The problem is that the Republicans, as bad as they are, are only slowing down progressive development—globalization, free trade, open borders, citizenship of the world, income equality, wealth redistribution, and community ownership of everything. Democrats, on the other hand, by coincidence or by design, will destroy this country.

The good news is that most of our political problems have economic solutions, and this book makes it easy, even for someone with an average education to understand how the economy functions and why we need a major reform of our financial system. Now it is up to Democrats to decide between advocating for such a reform or to continue with old ways of doing things.

CAPITAL VERSUS LABOR

The exploitation of the working class has been one of the major propaganda points of American left for over a century. Exploitation means that workers are paid lower wages than they deserve. All Democratic presidential candidates promise to take on those big, bad corporations, and empower labor unions to get a fair shake, which means higher wages, better healthcare, bigger pensions, etc. Labor costs are passed on to the consumer, and in the end, it is the consumer who pays for higher cost of production. This is extortion, and it is not good for the economy for many reasons.

First, this extortion demonstrates that American workers are paid not based on the free market but on ability to extort more money —strikes, slowdowns, etc.

Second, it is a moral question. Any benevolent dictator can reasonably argue that in a democracy conventional morality reflects the interests of the strong. Organized labor has been organized for the purpose of extorting more money than they would be paid in a free market. In the end, low wage workers pay more than a fair price for goods produced by unionized labor. Since economic justice is very questionable in any democracy where labor unions exist, democracies cannot reasonably claim higher moral ground.

The third reason is that when business owners pay extortion wages and benefits, they usually have less money left over to invest in expansion or improvement of the business. The result is the slow accumulation of capital—plant, equipment, machinery, etc. Of all of the reasons, the last one is the most damaging.

To increase the standard of living, we have to produce more. To produce more, we need to invest in automation and robots. To invest, businesses need money. Money—internal funds—come from profits. The higher the profits are, the better the opportunities for investment are, which means a higher standard of living for the whole of society. Democrats agitate for higher wages and lower profits, which means lower investment, lower productivity and, ultimately, a lower standard of living and more poverty.

When businesses lack internal funds for investment, they use external financing; they issue shares of stock, or sell bonds, or borrow from banks. Our tax code favors debt; interest is deductible. An average corporation is loaded with debt, and the credit rating is just one notch above junk. The liquidation of debt will start sooner or later. It will become clear that accumulation of insane levels of debt brought a lot of temporary prosperity. It would have been much wiser to crush labor unions and use internal funds instead of debt.

Workers benefit from accumulation of capital regardless of who owns that capital – government in the Marxist socialist system or the class of capitalists in a capitalist system. Workers do not own anything in either of the two systems.

TARIFFS AS A COST ON CHINESE EXPORTERS

President Trump described tariffs as a cost to Chinese exporters. The media says the tariffs are additional costs, and American consumers will pay more. Who is right?

Imagine for a minute that you have stage-3 cancer, but if you agree to undergo treatment you will lose your hair. What would you rather lose, your life or your hair?

Trade with China is a case of a malignant cancer killing our economy. Chinese communists deserve a Nobel Prize in economics for their brilliance in economic strategy. They see Pax Americana as a Dumb Empire to be destroyed economically with the help of media and commodity traders. Chinese communists are exporting cheap manufactured goods and choking our manufacturing sector to death. To avoid death, companies are moving production to China. The Chinese direct their companies to buy agricultural goods from America, which provides subsidies to its farmers so that they sell agricultural goods to China at lower prices. This is how we are destroying our manufacturing sector and subsidizing Chinese communists and their military. There is no doubt about the trend. If President Trump does not increase tariffs gradually to at least 200%, then by 2050 this country will become an agricultural colony of China.

And who will pay for high tariffs? China. We will choke their exports down to the right size, which in this book is equal to a nice round number: $100 billion. Now the media can calculate how much or how little high tariffs—200% minimum—will cost Chinese exporters, and how many jobs will be created in this country in the manufacturing sector.

A DRAGON AGAINST A PAPER TIGER

Mao Zedong, the leader of Communist Party of China from 1949 to 1976, used to call America "a paper tiger." Since then, not much has changed. If you Google the phrase "exported agricultural goods and imported manufactured goods," you will most likely find examples of developing countries trading with their colonial masters a long time ago. Today, China is threatening to increase tariffs on American goods—corn, soybeans, pork, and other agricultural stuff. We have about a $500 billion trade deficit with China. President Trump increased tariffs on Chinese goods aiming to reduce the trade deficit by $100 billion. This is, of course, the first step, because a $400 billion trade deficit is not much better. We should also stop agricultural subsidies, because agricultural subsidies allow farmers to sell their goods at low prices to China, and in the end, we subsidize China and their military. Our goals should be zero export of agricultural goods to China, zero export of high technology to China, and balanced trade.

On a fundamental level, we do not need any trade with China. America cannot produce everything. The United States buys coffee, cacao, tropical fruits and spices, etc. on the world market, but we should not buy high-tech goods from China, because without protectionist tariffs all production will move to China, where wages are five times lower. And what if our trade with China is reduced to zero? It will be very beneficial for the United States. We will no longer be an agricultural colony of China. Instead of growing food for China we will be able to use our labor force to build modern new cities. Agricultural production is not very friendly for our environment. Manure from animal farms, pesticides, all kinds of chemicals... Why do we need it? To reduce trade deficit with China? There is a very simple, clean, and efficient way to reduce trade deficit with China—tax the imports!

Both major political parties of the United States must work together to protect our economy. We can have free trade with our allies in Europe, but to finance the Chinese military is pure insanity.

THE ARMS RACE

By now, it should be clear to everyone that the world is entering a new Cold War. The old Cold War was easy to understand. The Soviet Union wanted to dominate the world by spreading Marxist ideology. First China, and later Russia, both Marxist, and both embraced capitalism. President Obama famously blundered by assuming that another cold war between America and Russia was impossible because Russia was no longer a Marxist state. Obama, a constitutional lawyer, obviously, did not study the history of Russia.

One should ask what China and Russia want? Both despise the American leadership of the free world; both despise America's form of government, America's efforts to spread democracy around the world; and both are preparing to challenge America militarily. Both China and Russia see American democracy as a weakness, as a deadly disease that sooner or later will cause a collapse of the empire. They smell blood in the water. The sharks are circling. Perceived weakness attracts aggression. China is already pushing America out of Asia. Russia is pushing America out of Europe.

Fortunately for us, China and Russia, even though both are blinded by their hatred for America and dreaming about the destruction of our pesky empire, cannot easily form a really strong military alliance. A few centuries ago, Russia occupied and annexed a huge territory from the Ural Mountains to the Pacific Ocean. That territory was populated by various Asian ethnic groups who were related to the Chinese people. If America is destroyed as a superpower, the next deadly fight will take place between China and Russia, but that worry is a long way down the road. In the short and medium-term the two adversaries are more than willing to form a tactical alliance against America, with goals for China to dominate Asia, and for Russia to dominate Europe.

Russia's first goal is to disband NATO, or at least to push all European countries out of military alliance with America. With America pushed out, NATO will become RATO, with Russia providing security and collecting tribute in hard currency for common defense against America. With collected "voluntary" contributions, Putin's band of oligarchs will take control of the most valuable assets in Europe. This would be the fastest way to modernize Russia, and to restore the great Russian empire. Russia will continue to bully and harass Ukraine to demonstrate that America is a paper tiger. The logic here is, you are not going to risk a nuclear war protecting Ukraine, are you?

The most rational solution would be for Ukraine to submit to the annexation of Crimea and the occupied part of Ukraine. After that we should admit Ukraine into NATO to prevent further dismemberment of that country.

China, not to be left behind, occupied a number of islands in the South China Sea that were claimed by Japan and other countries in the region. The Obama administration was so busy apologizing for past and present crimes of American imperialism, so bent on projecting soft power and charming the world that they did not even notice that China was spending more than America on defense. Because wages in China are five times lower than in America, in dollar terms, $150 billion in China is equivalent to $750 billion in America, but American economists, occupied with fancy theories, either never paid attention to this problem, or just don't care. Talking heads on TV only say that America's defense budget is three times bigger than China's and Russia's combined.

The worst part is that America should not blame anyone but itself. America dug the hole, in which it is now trapped. America allowed China to become rich by opening its market to Chinese goods and selling valuable technologies in exchange for promises of a "win-win situation" in the future. Well, the future has arrived, and America lost. Now is the time to stop the losses. We cannot be in an arms race with China, and continue to sell technologies with military applications to China at the same time. Even ordinary trade—shoes, clothing, etc.—allows China to earn dollars and to finance their arms race. That is why there is no alternative to high tariffs and trade wars. Talking heads on TV will whine about trade wars and lost profits, but ordinary Americans should understand that vital interests of this country are more important than profits of globalists. If we manage to restrict the flow of money to the governments of China and Russia, they will have less money for the arms race, and we will also need lower taxes to finance the arms race. Otherwise, we will need either to increase taxes or to start printing money. At the present time China is getting rich from trade with America. With a mountain of American dollars, China is buying advanced military technology from Russia. The income from selling advanced military technology to China is financing military—industrial complex of Russia. In effect, America is subsidizing military- industrial complexes of both China and Russia.

In his General theory, Keynes argued that the capitalist economy had "fundamentals flaws," chief among them being the excessively unequal distribution of income and the inability to maintain full employment. Keynes advocated for the "*euthanasia of the rentier*," meaning a decrease in the capital share of the total income and the socialization of investment. He blames the scarcity of capital for our inability to maintain full employment. In hindsight, Keynes made a major contribution to economic theory by advocating for a more active role of government in managing the business cycle, but his policy prescriptions were weak and ineffective. There was only one way to give the government tools for managing the economy—to abandon the gold standard, start printing currency, and to make what Irving Fisher called "productive loans." We can only guess why neither Keynes nor Fisher called for abandoning the gold standard, but the most likely reason was that the idea of printing paper currency not backed by gold would have been too radical for that time. Irving Fisher at least offered a detailed explanation of how the liquidation of debt leads to an economic depression. Now, in the

21st century, a determined government, if it owns and controls the central bank, has all the tools to prevent a severe economic depression. This means that Keynes was wrong. It was not that capitalism was flawed; it was that the banking system based on the gold standard was flawed. Actually, the banking system is still inherently unstable. A handful of big banks have an ability to start the liquidation of debt and knock the economy down into an economic depression, but now we at least understand the mechanism.

This book advocates for the creation of a central bank owned and controlled by the federal government. There are two main reasons. First, we need the ability to make emergency loans to big banks in large amounts—billions of dollars—if and when there is a financial panic and a run on the banks. The fractional reserve principle is a fact of life. The commercial banks cannot meet even a 10% withdrawal in cash from deposits, and it is not their fault.

The second major reason is the need to finance construction of modern new cities. Millions of Americans live with their parents into their 30s because they cannot afford to buy or rent a decent apartment. Most politicians do not understand that we need to build more housing. Democrats are pushing for "living wages" so that the working poor will have more money to pay rent. Rent control does not help either. If you forced chicken farmers to sell their chickens for even 5% lower than normal, many farmers will reduce production, the supply of chickens will go down, and the market price of chickens will go up. Instead of lower prices consumers will pay higher prices. The same logic applies to apartments. Rent control makes real estate investments unattractive. The result is low supply and higher prices to buy or rent. The correct solution is to increase the supply of real estate.

The federal government owns about 50% of land in our Western States. Why not sell some of that land for low prices with the condition that the buyers build modern new cities? The central bank can provide construction loans at low interest rates. Selling land at below-market prices and providing construction loans at below free market interest rates will reduce costs of construction, and real estate will be sold at affordable prices. The federal government provides subsidies to the agricultural industry so that farmers can sell soybeans to China at lower prices. America slowly but surely is becoming an agricultural colony of China, and American taxpayers are even subsidizing these destructive processes. This policy of agricultural subsidies is beyond foolish. Why not subsidize a much more beneficial policy to build modern new cities? In return, real estate developers should agree to sell real estate in subsidized new cities at prices only 1% higher than cost. If one city block cost, say, $4 billion to build, then 1% will be about $40 million of guaranteed profit.

At the present time we build around one million homes in the United States annually. We need to gradually increase the construction industry's capacity so that we can build two million apartments in the modern new cities every year. How many jobs can we create? If an average worker is paid $30,000 a year, and an average apartment costs $300,000 to build, including the cost of infrastructure, then construction of one apartment creates 10 jobs for one year. It means that construction of 1 million apartments every year will create 10 million jobs for one year. If we manage to build 2 million apartments every year, it will create 20 million jobs per year, and it will be reasonably permanent jobs, without on-again off-again instability.

The subprime mortgage crisis exposed the criminal mentality of not only the Wall Street sharks, but that of our financial system in general. Investors all over the world lost billions of dollars. They lost faith in democratic capitalism in the American-led world order. We lost our moral superiority. We have descended to the level of those who we used to lecture about democracy and the rule of law, but America cannot lead from the moral bottom. It is time to clean up. The American financial system is a good place to start if we want to prolong the American Century.

Please visit www.globalpovertysolution.com

All proceeds from this book go to a charity

www.ingramcontent.com/pod-product-compliance
Lightning Source LLC
Chambersburg PA
CBHW071618150726
48000CB00004B/1774